On the Yeti Trail

The Search for the Elusive Snowman

On the Yeti Trail

The Search for the Elusive Snowman

Tribhuvan Nath
Madan M. Gupta

UBSPD
UBS Publishers' Distributors Ltd.
New Delhi Bombay Bangalore Madras
Calcutta Patna Kanpur London

UBS Publishers' Distributors Ltd.
5 Ansari Road, New Delhi-110 002
Bombay Bangalore Madras Calcutta
Patna Kanpur London

First Published 1994

Cover design : UBS Art Studio

Lasertypeset in 11 pt. Times at Alphabets, New Delhi and printed at Pauls Press, Okhla New Delhi

Imagined sketch of the abominable snowman by an artist.

Imagined sketch of the abominable snowman by an artist.

To
The eternal lust
for knowing
what should not be known

Preface

Frankly speaking, the accounts given by several Nepalese and foreign climbers on the yeti are the products of my co-author's (Madan Mohan Gupta's) sweat and toil, and his original and exclusive contributions to this volume are gratefully acknowledged. He was, as I have personally witnessed, on intimate terms with Tenzing Norgay and Norbu, big shots among Sherpa climbers. Gupta had travelled extensively in the Nepal Himalayas to such remote and inaccessible places as Mustang, the Nepalese enclave in Tibet, and Namche Bazar on the foothills of the Everest range. Such travelling was accomplished partly on pony, negotiating bridle paths along hairpin bends of precipices, promontories and cliffs, and partly on canoes to cross turbulent mountain streams. He had also known the hospitality of the tribals of Helmu (Helumbu), located at a few days' march from Kathmandu.

Gupta would interact with Sherpas through Nepal-based Lamas, who knew Nepali or Hindi. I did visit a few Tibetan homes in and around Kathmandu along

9

with Gupta, but my ignorance of Tibetan dialects stood as a barrier to my comprehension of his conversations with his hosts. Dom Moraes, the Booker Award winner, who visited Nepal, speaks warmly in *Gone Away* about Gupta; so do several Swiss and British mountaineers in the accounts of their expeditions to the various Nepalese peaks.

Gupta wanted his account on living yetis to be published before the creature was actually found. A few of the visiting Western press correspondents who saw his script advised him to modify and recast it because, in their opinion, it was worth publication. However, Gupta could not give the 'finishing touches' to his copy as he was handicapped by a certain unfortunate ailment in his throat which forced him to snore and doze off while standing, talking or typing. I had made a commitment to him to complete his unfinished job (on both his volumes) as best as I could, but my preoccupation with reporting for Indian dailies left me very little time. One part of my job involved retrieving the yeti search stories from the extant 'blacks' of Gupta's news cables and the other part in editing his yeti stories that now appear as part two of this book, the first posthumous publication of several individuals' accounts of their encounters with the abominable snowman.

Gupta had a natural sense of humour and, moreover, he was an excellent raconteur. As I pored over his yellowed scripts, I developed a curiosity about our redoubtable tailless ancestor, immortalised by Charles Darwin. Over a period of more than two decades, I collected a large number of newspaper clippings on the yeti. My effort in the first two chapters is aimed at updating selective accounts of various sightings of the yeti and climbers' testimonies on the abominable snowman as glimpsed in the far-flung corners of the earth. In my attempt at rewriting, I have avoided distortion and ignored mutilations, if illegible, in Gupta's typescript. Indeed, I am solely responsible for errors which may have crept in inadvertently.

The merit of Gupta's account lies in demolishing the then prevailing scepticism about the yeti's existence by reproducing first-person accounts of men and women who had encountered the yeti.

But for Mrs. Chandravati Gupta's insistence and unfailing help, I could hardly have placed this material before readers, both sceptic and knowledgeable.

Acknowledgement is also due to Ms Maureen E. Pawers, a US Peace Corps volunteer, posted in Nepal in 1968, for pencil sketches of the imagined identity of the yeti.

In recent years, scientists have collected sufficient evidence to describe the physiognomy of different species of the abominable snowman as found at different places on the earth. Though the yeti was not considered fit enough to be mentioned in any standard publication till the sixties, this creature eventually found its way into the *Encyclopaedia of the Unexplained*[1] published from London.

Scientists debating about the yeti's existence are broadly divisible into two camps, the 'believers' and the 'non-believers'. Opinions voiced from both camps have been cited in the first two chapters, i.e., my contribution. In the face of these opinions, one cannot assert that the monstrous biped of the Himalayas is absolutely non-existent. Indeed, more positive proof is required. Public scepticism on this score must come to an end. Given the advantage of night vision devices, zoom lenses and electronic gadgets, it may not be difficult to give the yeti a chase and trap or photograph it in its natural habitat, though man cannot surpass the yeti in climbing mountains. Till the yeti's existence and identity are unequivocally confirmed, the reader may feel free to choose the camp he or she would like to belong to.

The abominable snowman, who could possibly be the missing link, appears to be a survivor of the Ice Age *Gigantopitheous*, fossil fragments of whose lower jawbone and teeth were discovered in Haritalyangar in the vicinity of a lake in district Bilaspur of Himachal Pradesh, a mountainous state of North India. Such a discovery was made by a joint team of the Punjab and Yale Universities way back in the sixties. Apparently, the glacial period mammal migrated from the Himalayas to Pamir and Caucasus and Europe in the West, and to Mongolia, Gobi, China and Siberia, and thence to Alaska and southward to the Rockies and the Andes.

Tribhuvan Nath

Notes and References

1. Richard Cavendish(ed.), *Encyclopaedia of the Unexplained: Magic, Occultism and Parapsychology.* (See Select Bibliography for further details, *in all cases.*)

Contents

Preface   9
Introduction   15

PART I : Placing the Yeti in Perspective
1. Sightings of the Yeti   21
2. The Dark Secret of the Himalayas   39

**PART II : Individual Testimonies
(Gathered by Madan M. Gupta between 1957
and 1968)**
3. A Close Brush with the Yeti:
   As told by Yogi Narahari Nath   61
4. Abducted into a Yeti's Cave   65
5. Ma-Yu's Escape from a Yeti   71
6. I Became a Yeti's Wife   76

PART III : Appendices
Appendix 1 : Excerpts from Brian
              S.N. Ashkenazi's Letter   91
Appendix 2 : Ashkenazi's Encounter with
              the *Jangli Admi*   93
Appendix 3 : Ashkenazi's Version of Two
              Yeti Species   95
Appendix 4 : Excerpt from Naya Sandesh
              (Weekly)   96

Appendix 5 : Yeti or the Snowman   98
Appendix 6 : Summary of Jeanne
                       Koffman's Report   104
Appendix 7 : China's Version of Abominable
                       Snowman   107
Epilogue   108
Select Bibliography   120

Introduction

I

Science does not give credence to the existence of ghosts and fairies; it demands foolproof evidence. Such evidence about the existence of the mysterious creature known as the *yeti* (and to the West as the abominable snowman) of Nepal is still lacking. Yet, a gullible public fed on yarns is reluctant to disbelieve the existence, in the Himalayas, of a primordial creature which is hardly ever visible. What has been fuelling speculation about its identity is the fortuitous sighting of a biped's giant-size footprints on snow in the remote and inaccessible mountain ranges of Nepal. These footprints provide the only clue to the existence of a gigantic creature, an apeman — maybe the primeval man — who shuns human society and prefers to dwell aloof.

Prolonged intervals have separated the various sightings of the yeti in the past 166 years. Each individual sighting has triggered off worldwide sensation, followed by an uncanny silence among explorers, mountain climbers, anthropologists, scientists, including zoologists. If they ever suspected that the creature of their imagined identity was non-existent, the emergence

15

of fresh footprints each time has posed a new challenge to their investigative acumen.

Though very few have actually caught a glimpse of this bizarre creature, the scientific community's scepticism about its existence has now gradually given way to half-belief, partly based on half-truth and partly on untruth. The first clue to the existence of such a mysterious creature surfaced in the nineteenth century in the Gobi desert (Mongolia). Further, about a hundred years ago, a Western explorer named L. A. Waddel sighted enormous footprints near a place called Donkyla on the Nepal-Tibet border. Over the past four decades, mountaineers and explorers have gathered enough evidence about the existence of this creature in three northern continents. Even then, certain scientists are inclined to treat the yeti as a figment of imagination. The chapters that follow seek to sift absurd fiction from bald reality about this creature.

After World War II, the Western mountaineering teams went footloose over the giant snow-bound peaks on the Nepal-Tibet border. They brought back, apart from their accounts of failure or success, the weird tales of a shadowy creature whose unseen visit was manifested in the footprints it had left around their high-altitude camps.

II

Monsters, genii, evil spirits and sweet angels figure in the folklore of almost every country and civilisation. Britain has its Loch Ness monster; China and Tibet have their dragons; and Nepal, Sikkim and Bhutan their yeti, in tune with their pastoral fancy. In modern times, flying saucers and 'visitors from outer space' have swelled the list of myths baffling humanity. Be it a *hallucinatory object*, a *relict humanoid* or a *Homo nocturna*, as known to the naturalists, the yeti's actual sighting is regarded as ominous by the natives of the Nepal Himalayas. If the natives shun this filthy creature, whose presence exudes a foul stink, the yeti itself dreads smoke or fire-carrying objects as it possesses an inflammable coat of thick fur. It vanishes in a trice at the sight of man. The yeti can instinctively sniff human presence from a distance. Indeed, mysterious tales about the yeti abound in the folklore of Nepal. The native Sherpas, however, never had a shred of doubt about its existence, and they do not view him as a spook or evil spirit.

III

Endowed with a fervid sixth sense, one of the authors, namely, Madan Mohan Gupta, a Kathmandu-based journalist and cameraman, set himself solus on the yeti trail in the wake of the Western climbers' accounts of the huge footprints apparently belonging to what they called the 'abominable snowman.' In the nineteen sixties M. M. Gupta was for nine years the contemporary of the other author (Tribhuvan Nath) when he was posted as *The Times of India* correspondent in Nepal.

Following Gupta's untimely and sudden death in January 1971, his widow Chandravati Gupta, shifted to her parents' home at Patna. In keeping with her husband's oft-repeated wish, she mailed to the second author a sheaf of dog-eared carbon copies of his cables and stories on the yeti. Another bunch of his stories relate to anecdotes of the fabulous Rana times. They cover a period when the mountain kingdom was a Shangrila, in the real sense of the word, out of bounds for foreigners. Gupta had interviewed members of virtually every mountaineering expedition to the Nepal Himalayas during a period of nearly 25 years, specifically on the riddle of the yeti's existence. His news stories were splashed in the Western and Indian newspapers. Also, he recorded the views of leading contemporary theologians, both Hindu and Buddhist, on what their scriptures had to say about this creature.

At one time in the late nineteen forties and early fifties, Gupta enjoyed a virtual monopoly of all political and mountaineering news emanating from Nepal. Initially, when the kingdom was closed to foreigners, he was operating from his hometown Raxaul, the gateway to southern Nepal.

Part I

Placing the Yeti
in Perspective

Part 1

Placing the Veil
in Perspective

1

Sightings of the Yeti

*"... There is nothing in this world so strange
as to be truly unbelievable ..."*

Bernard Levin in *The Belle and the Bird*, quoted in
The Statesman, 2 May 1993

The Himalayas in northern Nepal offer one of the most
exquisite and breath-taking views on earth. The
spectacular vastness of the eternally snow-covered
expanse displays its inviolate infinity of space, its
immense emptiness and silent serenity. A panorama
without a match the landscape resembles a broad
staircase, rising steeply northward to a multitude of
giant-size snow-bound peaks that seem to merge with
the clouds. Neither a single shred of vegetation nor a
trace of *Hazrat-e-Adam's* (mankind) habitat is visible
anywhere. Even avian life seems to find repose as the
treeline stands dwarfed below. Under a cloud-free sky,
one can verily visualise what the ancient rishis described
as the 'Nagadhiraj Himalaya' (the abode of snow,
crowned with jewels). The sole element dominating the
scene is the all-pervasive silence, broken intermittently by
furious snowstorms, terrible gales and the raucous roar
of cracking avalanches. At times, one can observe nature
in her cruellest moods "where", to quote a Western
mountaineer, "the earth surging upwards thrusts herself
— stark, bleak and lonely".

21

On the Yeti Trail

Nearly 200 towering peaks, including Mt. Everest and Kanchenjunga, to name just two, seem vying with each other to kiss the sky. Scattered in a confused pattern along the 1200-km Nepal–Tibet border, these lofty ranges constitute a grim, formidable barrier to human effort.

For long stretches the rocky mountains and valleys are covered with a thick blanket of dazzling white snow. At places, the white ice glitters like crystals under the impact of sun rays. It is similar to a polar landscape where nothing is visible apart from snow as far as the sight can reach. There are indeed exceptions, although rare, on the niches of a few snow-bound ranges, where nature has conceded some space to tiny settlements of local tribes, totally cut off from the civilised world for the better part of the year. Left to fend for themselves these people betray an instinctive 'gift of the gab'. They relieve their humdrum life of monotony by gossiping about monsters and fairies. Theirs is a pastoral world of make-believe in which mysteries enliven the dull moments of life.

Although the present writer (Tribhuvan Nath) spent nearly a decade in Nepal, he did not ever have the occasion to trek over this sector of the Himalayas. He merely got a glimpse of this snow-clad land from the portholes of an aircraft which had been pressed into service by the Royal Nepal Airlines Corporation for some tourists' flight along the Everest range. It is this terrain which is supposed to provide a hideout to the abominable snowman.

Half-man, half-beast, the tailless, hairy biped, familiar to Nepalese Sherpa highlanders by the name of yeti, remains one of the world's most illusive mysteries. It's a riddle whether the creature is a myth or reality; an enigma whether it is man or beast; and an inscrutable mystery whether it is 'the missing link'. It hardly ever had any 'address' on earth although it has been 'dropping' its 'visiting card' near the high-altitude climbers' camps in the shape of enormous footprints on snow. These footprints present a bizarre phenomenon in that that they are always sighted by chance. They resemble human footprints with one anatomical difference inasmuch as its owner's sole protrudes with four splayed toes and the fifth turned backward.

In Nepal, the rarely visible monster, credited with a superhuman size, is known to Sherpas as 'Meito Kangmi' (*Mi* means man and *Kang*, snow), or the filthy dweller of the snow, which literally translated by Western explorers, became the 'abominable snowman'.

Lacking concrete proof, scientists have been circumspect about the existence of this creature, although several climbing expeditions have repeatedly sighted footprints at altitudes where no human being dare walk barefoot on the snow. The sightings have convinced expedition leaders that one day the century-old search for the elusive snowman will yield positive results. People among the high-altitude tribes of Nepal, notably the Sherpas, renowned for their climbing stamina, have an inexhaustible repertoire of yarns about their Meito Kangmi's real identity, though they have no concrete evidence except legends.

Anyone living in the Sherpa land at the foot of Mt. Everest will affirm that the yeti is a reality. According to one writer: "Why not? The dreaded monster visited the village on the other side of their mountain range on several nights. The natives have a penchant for playing a hoax on the 'white Saheb log' interested in having a handshake with their ancestor(?) "

Until the nineteen sixties, scientists used to reject, with sneers of disbelief, all talk of the yeti's existence.

Specimens of scalps, skin, hair, the skeletal hand of a yeti (preserved in a monastery) and excrements collected from snow-bound rock caves have been brought back after intensive search by field investigators belonging to different nationalities. Such specimens have been examined in Western laboratories and discarded as unreliable evidence. Regardless of failures, it remains today a dream nurtured by many explorers, naturalists, zoologists and anthropologists to lift the veil of mystery over the yeti's existence. So far, none has succeeded though the creature has come sensationally close to 'discovery'.

Yeti Locations

To establish that the 'abominable snowman' is a reality, the believers have got to produce irrefutable evidence. A photograph of the yeti scalp (kept in Khumjung monastery) is now in the safe custody of the Nepal Mountaineering Club. More clues to the yeti's existence were made available to mountaineers from an isolated region called Mustang, which juts into Tibetan territory. A yeti was once reported to have been killed here, while a skeleton of the creature was discovered in a crevasse in Tarke Khola, located in this area. Other locations that have attracted the climbers looking for the yeti are Tachi Lepka Pass (situated at 19,100 ft. or about 5080 m); the upper Dudh Kosi valley besides Bar Bung Khola in the vicinity of Dhaulagiri mountain.

A number of places in the Everest region are associated with the yeti phenomenon. Among them, Iswa Khola is known as the 'yeti land'. Another tract which attracts most of the yeti hunters is the Barun Valley in the vicinity of the Everest and Makalu ranges. This is known as the Mahalangur Himal (the mountain of the great monkey).

To the south of the foot of Mt. Everest, one comes across two ancient monasteries at Thyangboche and Pangboche whose lamas (monks) have occasionally whetted the climbers' curiosity about the yeti by giving them weird accounts of the creature. A yeti scalp has been preserved in the Pangboche monastery and another one in Khumjung (as already mentioned). A photograph of the latter scalp was taken by the veteran climber, G.W. Schulchess, since the monks refused to part with the original.

The yeti's sporadic movements have been reported from places far apart on the Himalayas — from Kashmir to Arunachal Pradesh through Kumayun, Garhwal, Nepal and Sikkim. Rarely, if ever, has the yeti come close enough to be photographed by the climbers' cameras. Its presence has also been reported from Tibet and the Hubei provinces (in China).

Yeti Sightings (in Chronological Order)

In the nineteenth century, one Colonel Nikolai Prsvalsky, a Russian explorer, reported the presence of the 'abominable snowman' in the Gobi desert of Mongolia[1].

A long gap separates L.A. Waddel's discovery of the yeti footprints in 1899 on the Nepal–Tibet border from Henry Elwes's reference to the abominable snowman in 1914. Waddel, who was a botanist exploring in the Himalayas, sighted the creature's footprints near Donkyala on the Tibet side of the Nepal–Tibet border.

Again, in 1921, Lt. Col. C. K. Howard Bury chanced upon the yeti's footprints during the first-ever British reconnaissance of the Everest region from the Tibet side. N. A. Tonbazi, a Greek botanist, saw the footprints in 1925 near Zemu Pass in Sikkim.

In 1938, Brian Samelovich Ashkenazi, (see Appendix 1 for details) a resident of Bombay, managed to observe the abominable snowman at close quarters outside the Peshawar Cantonment railway station, though he disclosed "his secret" perhaps for the first time only in 1981!

Climbing expeditions to the Himalayas were interrupted by World War II. They were resumed after the war, and Sherpa Tenzing Norgay reported having seen yeti footprints in 1946 while engaged in a reconnaissance of the Everest region for a British team.

It was Eric Shipton's Everest reconnaissance party that saw distinct footprints for the first time on the Menlung glacier in the Everest region.

In the Fifties and Sixties

The mid-fifties saw a train of expeditions comprising different nationalities 'raiding' Nepalese peaks to catch the snowman dead or alive. Hunter dogs and equipment such as cameras with telephoto lenses, tranquilliser guns and nylon ropes were used by the expeditionists to aid the search. But the camera shutter grease was said to have frozen at that altitude and dogs of a breed credited for high altitude stamina shed their DNA on the snowscape.

Ralph Izzard's Yeti hunting expedition[2], spent five months (February—May 1954) in the Solu-Khumbu districts located in the foothills of Mt. Everest where its members, short of locating the yeti, scaled eight peaks exceeding altitudes of 18,000 ft. (about 5450 m), which included Kangso Shar (19,950 ft.), Pokalda (19,050 ft.) and Hongu (south) peak (20,013 ft.). The adventurers later trekked to Pu Mori, the site of the Indian climbers' highest camp that season.

That very year a Japanese climbing expedition to Manaslu peak, led by Y. Hotta, went to Ganesh Himal (24,299 ft.) supposed to be the native habitat of the elusive yeti in the Nepal Himalayas. This expedition also tried, but in vain, to locate the dweller of snow caverns.

The 1955 mountaineering season in Nepal attracted a Franco-Swiss team to climb Ganesh Himal. The Swiss climber, Raymond Lambert, who led this multinational team, was not inclined to believe in the existence of the yeti. His Belgian teammate, Canon Jules Detry, held a different view. (See various versions cited in the following chapter.)

In January 1956 at Tadadege, a village on the Indo—Tibetan border, an abominable snowman was reported to have been killed in the Siang district of Arunachal Pradesh. The political officer of the district informed a party of visiting journalists at Along that the creature had been killed by tribals.

William Grant, a confirmed believer in the yeti, preferred two aspects of the yeti riddle — one regarding the Russian finding of a gigantic anthropoid in the Pamirs and the other indicating that a giant hominid, known to anthropologists as *Gigantopithecus*, used to roam the Himalayas in the Stone Age. Later, this hominid has believed to have migrated to other regions of the snow-clad mountains in neighbouring China and Myanmar (Burma).

"I have no doubt," stated Grant "that the yeti exists." He had spent his best years searching for the yeti which could have been found in mountain forests rather than near peaks.

Jan Frostis and Aage Thorberg, two Norwegian mountaineers, scouring the Nepal Himalayas, had earlier conveyed to the Nepalese Government a report narrating how a member of their party was knocked down by a huge ape-like hairy creature when they followed the track of a snowman.

On the Yeti Trail

Among the members of the Everest expedition (1953), Charles Evans did not hold a brief for the existence of the abominable snowman although the team leader, Sir John Hunt hoped that it would be found one day.

In 1955, an expedition comprising Gerald Russell and Norman Dyrhenfurth, the Texan oil tycoon, undertook a search for the yeti around Everest and Makalu regions. Between September and December, its members trekked in Barun Valley along with their hunter dogs. A Sherpa member of the team sighted the yeti. A chase by trained dogs failed to catch the yeti as the former developed high-altitude sickness.

On returning to Kathmandu, Dyrhenfurth said, "We want to declare that the yeti is no more a myth. We will have the truth." He collected from the Buddhist monastery at Khumjung a skeletal hand which its Tibetan lama owner ascribed to a yeti and a piece of dried skin (measuring 48" x 30") of an animal unknown to science.

Two American teams made several forays within a span of two years from January 1957 to September 1958. Led by Tom Slick, the first team stayed on the mountains from January to March 1957. Unwilling to abandon the search, Slick got his stay extended till July and scoured the Everest base region. He persisted in bitter cold till December, looking for clues to the presence of the shy, withdrawn creature.

A third American expedition was headed by Peter Byrnes and was sponsored by the San Antonio Zoological Society of California. It wanted to trek to Nangpa La *en route* to Tibet. Since 1954, his was the fifth expedition to the Nepal Himalayas, aimed at tracking down the abominable snowman. Its members included Brian Byrnes, Kirk Johnson (junior) and Bach Ketti of the Indian Zoological Society.

Peter Byrnes declared on returning to Kathmandu: "We are convinced that the yeti must be found one day."

The outcome of the two-year search by the Slick–Johnson expedition was the collection of (1) a century-old dried hand from Khumjung monastery, (2) a photograph of the scalp of a creature which was alive a century earlier (preserved in the Thyangboche monastery), (3) a skin supposed to belong to a child yeti, (4) droppings from a cave, and (5) pastoral yarns about the yeti.[3]

The foregoing efforts were followed by the Japanese Jugal Himal expedition (1959–61) and the Japanese Keio University expedition led by K. Kato. Members of the university expedition to Dhaulagiri II (25,429 ft.) sighted the footprints of a minor yeti, which was called Miteh by their Sherpa mates. The length of the footprints did not exceed five inches.

In November 1959, Giavano Spani, a representative of Italian Television and *Il Tempo*, an Italian journal, went to the Furte Lekpa region in search of the yeti; nothing tangible emerged from his endeavours.

The luckiest of the lot was perhaps a person who had not gone to search for the yeti but had a chance encounter with a twelve-foot giant. This person was Yogi Narhari Nath, contemporary Nepal's noted Sanskrit scholar and Himalayan traveller, who sighted the giant as he was trekking back home from Lake Mansarovar (Tibet). (An interview with Yogi Narhari Nath along with his statement appears later in this book.) This 'chance encounter' stimulated a revival of interest in the yeti's existence when foreign expeditionists had almost lost all hope.

In 1959, two more expeditions tried unsuccessfully to search for the abominable snowman. They were the *Daily*

Mail yeti expedition led by Noel Barber, who went to Solu-Khumbu region to track down the creature. The other was a Japanese expedition commissioned by the Japanese Educational TV and the Mainichi Broadcasting System, and was led by Teizo Ogawa. Late in 1959, its members camped at an altitude of 11,486 ft. and scoured the nearby areas of Khumbu, Langmocha Khola, Lobujya Khola, Dudh Pokhari and Lhanjo for 50 days. Although they did not even see footprints of the yeti, Ogawa maintained: "We have returned convinced of the presence of an animal-like human being in the Himalayas which is more intelligent than a normal gorilla." The team brought back 10 specimens, including a piece of skin and a few bones of the yeti, for close scientific examination.

Edmund Hillary led an expedition to the Everest region in 1960 to track down the yeti. He camped in the Everest mountain and Lhanjo areas for fifty days. He found its footprints but remained sceptical about its existence. He borrowed from the Khumjung monastery what was supposed to be the preserved yeti scalp for scientific tests in Chicago. It afforded no clue to the existence of the enigmatic creature. Nevertheless, public curiosity was roused afresh when a Japanese team camping in the vicinity of Dhaulagiri mountain heard at night a shrill, whistling cry near its camp at a 5,100-metre altitude and at daybreak sighted the mysterious footprints on snow.

Expeditions to the Nepal Himalayas were suspended in the early sixties in the wake of Indo—China military engagements over the disputed Himalayan boundary.

In the Seventies
In the early seventies, mountaineering in Nepal attracted

fresh ventures from places far and near. The American Arun Valley wild life expedition undertook a field study of the yeti footprints in east Nepal Himalayas. Jeffrey McNeely, the joint leader of the expedition, acquired plaster casts of yeti footprints when the creature walked within a foot of their camp at night. The following day, Edward Cronin, the expedition's other joint leader, and Edward Emery, a zoologist and physician member of the team, saw a track on fresh snow at a 4000-metre altitude. Cronin was reported to have said at Boston: "I am not sure whether the yeti exists but available evidence points to the existence of an inquisitive ape-like animal in the forest dwellings of the Himalayas."[4]

Early in 1975, two Japanese climbing teams reported nocturnal intrusions by the abominable snowman near their high-altitude camps. The Sandai Alpine Club team that had gone to conquer Annapurna south peak (7219m.) sighted footprints on snow at a 5,170-m. altitude. The creature apparently went away as quietly as it had come.

Within the next few days, the Japanese Rock Climbing Society's expedition team to Dhaulagiri IV (7682m) reported hearing a weird sound resembling a human voice near its high-altitude camps. The sound was so loud that it alarmed the occupants of the camps. They found no trace of footprints when they launched a search in the morning but suspected that the voice that they had heard overnight was the abominable snowman's.

In neighbouring Sikkim, the State Government launched a yeti photographic expedition at 16000 ft. (nearly 5000 m) altitude in the vicinity of the National Park stretching from the river Zemu valley to Dzongri. Their efforts also came to nought.

In late seventies, a Kathmandu language tabloid

report disclosed that the progenies of a union between the yeti and human beings inhabiting Kaironja, Jhaling and Lapa in the Ganesh Himal region had sought Nepali citizenship. The *Naya Sandesh*, a Nepali weekly, quoted Hari Bahadur Thapa, a member of the Rashtriya Panchayat (National Assembly, now defunct) and Buddhiman Tamang, a member of Dhading District Panchayat (council), as saying that there exist such claimants for citizenship in their constituencies. (For a free translation of the tabloid's report, see Appendix 4.)

Outside the Himalayas

A noteworthy contemporary event was the discovery, in 1959, by the Soviet yeti expedition of the footprints of an unknown creature in the Blan Duik river basin in Pamir, north of Kashmir. This discovery apart, a species of an anthropoid frequenting the Caucasus attracted the attention of Russian scientists. According to a Soviet weekly journal, hundreds of people had sighted several species of wild hominid[5] in different mountainous Asian republics the erstwhile Soviet Union.

In the Caucasus region two 'unofficial' expeditions sent out by Jeanne Koffman[6], a scholar, a surgeon and a member of the then USSR Geographical Society, mentioned the presence of a wild creature in remote regions on the heights of the northern Caucasus and Pamirs. Reports of these expeditions were made public by Koffman in May 1978, whetting the readers' curiosity in the creature. Although Koffman said she had not seen the creature herself, an expedition member, Ruslan Shaminov, said he had sighted enormous footprints on 18 March 1975 in the valley of river Malka, 30 to 40 km from Mount Elbrus. Who or what could have left such superhuman footprints?

Between the fifties and the eighties scepticism about

the abominable snowman's existence yielded place to half-beliefs. What contributed to a reappraisal was the emergence of fresh evidence. Late in the eighties, a British physicist, Anthony B. Wooldridge, told an American Alpine Club meeting at New York that he had encountered a yeti in the course of his trek in the Himalayas. To substantiate his version, he exhibited two sets of photographs taken on 6 March 1986 on the Nepalese side of Nepal–Tibet border. One of these sets showed the mysterious tracks on snow made by the 'enormous feet splayed by big toes'. The second photograph, taken from a distance of 450 feet, shows a silhouette vaguely resembling a human being's. Both pieces of evidence were disputed by Grover S. Kranz, an anthropologist belonging to the Washington State University.[7]

Apart from the Himalayas and the Caucasus, the sighting of a creature resembling the abominable snowman was reported from remote mountainous sites in the United States of America.

Public curiosity was roused by the sighting of giant-size human footprints in a few remote places in the USA. These footprints lay scattered at different sites between Alaska and California.

Despite science's disbelief in fairies, ghosts and monsters, the aforementioned discoveries fired public imagination in the USA, where the mysterious creature was reported to have poached on chicken eggs and peered through glass windowpanes. The sightings indicated the distribution of this anthropoid in at least three continents.[8]

Creatures resembling the yeti in physiognomy were reported to have been sighted at a few places far apart from each other in Russia's Asian republics. Close to Verkhoyansk in the Yakut Valley, local people sighted several specimens of a hairy creature they call 'Chuchuma'.

Two female members of a Soviet amateur expedition team sighted a 'mysterious creature' in the Pamir-Ala mountain in Tadzikistan near a river bed.[10]

In 1981, B. S. Ashkenazi 'located a pair of yetis on the evening of 21 June on Pir Panjal, above Gulmarg, Kashmir' and sent a report of his finding along with photographs to the Kashmir Government.[11]

In the Eighties

In October 1984, at a Canton exhibition focussing on the search for the abominable snowman in China, one of the instances recounted was that of a herdsman kidnapped by a woman who looked like a bear and forced him to live with her in a Himalayan cave for seven years. She had two offspring by him. Another instance cited was that of a wild man who held a woman captive in Sichuan in south-western China for two years.[12] (Refer to the Nepalese woman's experience in the chapter ('I Became a Yeti's Wife'.)

Two Soviet scientific bodies gave contradictory verdicts on the existence of the abominable snowman. The Soviet Geographical Society analysed no fewer than 5000 descriptions of sightings of the Russian version of the abominable snowman which offer tell-tale evidence of the existence of this enigmatic creature. On the contrary, Vladimir Ratzec, a member of a commission set up by the Soviet Academy of Sciences to study the yeti question has expressed the view that the "creature is no longer alive".

In the Nineties

Two young German journalists — Jan Triebel and Andreas Schmalhofer attached to a Munich newspaper

— 'hiked and hunted' through Tibet and Nepal in the early nineties. One of their 'secret' objectives was to photograph the yeti or at least its footprints. In an article carried by *The Statesman*, 'Another Great Yeti Hunt', New Delhi, 8 February 1992, they also make a passing reference to the so-called yeti scalp preserved in the Khumjung monastery. Beginning from L. A. Waddel's discovery of the presence of a 'hairy, wild man' near Sikkim, the duo recall the outcome of the 1954 *Daily Mail* expedition to Nepal Himalayas and Edmund Hillary's search for the yeti in Khumbu. The Germans drew a blank but for the sighting of the scalps preserved in two monasteries. The German journalists also make a mention of the discovery of footprints at a 5770-metre-altitude by John Whyte's expedition in 1979 (location not specified). These measured 20.3cm in length and 10.1cm in width. According to them: "The creator of those footprints was estimated to have weighed 75 kg." In 1980, they cite a Polish climber's account testifying that he came across certain footprints at a 5770-metre altitude on his expedition's way up to the Everest summit. They observed that: "Like the rest, these prints featured a grossly splayed out big toe of the sort typical among monkeys." The Germans trekked through 'a landscape of massive peaks, colossal glaciers, tremendous passes and tiny but lively villages.' They also make a reference to the Alpinist and Tyrolean mountaineer's (Reinhold Messner) claim to be the first man in the world to have climbed every peak over 8000 metres in height. He had seen a yeti in the flesh in Tibet though, much to his regret, he had no camera when he saw it. The Germans did not come across footprints, despite valiant efforts. After citing all the local tales and the sighting of footprints by other climbers, they conclude that there was 'no tangible evidence of the yeti's existence.'

Odd footprints were sighted once again as recently as April 1992 in the autonomous republic of Karelia in Russia, according to the local newspaper *Severny Kuryer*. A DPA report[13] from Petrozavodsk cited the experience of a pensioner, one Victor Serikov and three of his friends, out on a fishing expedition on the banks of Svetloe lake nearly 50 km from the Karelian capital, Petrozavodsk. When they came back to their car to drink tea, they found that the thermos flask containing this beverage, and a packet of biscuits and sweets had vanished from the back seat. The fisherman 'found pieces of the broken flask nearby and next to them, the huge footprints of an unidentified creature'.

Serikov made a plate of the footprints whose dimensions were 41 cm in length and 20 cm in width. "It was found to be identical in size with that of another mystery snowman, nicknamed 'Yegor' by a local journalist who claimed to have found him."

Does the Yeti Exist?

Public curiosity about the mysterious creature's existence and identity is bound to persist as long as irrefutable proof is not available. Nevertheless, explorers and scientists have not abandoned the search. The British Broadcasting Corporation (BBC) is planning to send an expedition led by Brian Blessed (57), an actor, along with an eight-member crew, to make a televised adventure film on the search for the abominable snowman. The expedition has charted a 3000-mile itinerary through the Himalayas and the snowy wastes of Canada.

Brian Blessed also planned to mount a separate expedition to Mount Everest in August 1993 to answer the question as to whether the yeti is a myth or reality. The BBC expedition has been planned as a part of its televised travelogues.

Scientists refuse to accept the existence of the yeti in the absence of concrete, absolute proof. The mass of indirect evidence, collected by mountaineers, explorers and scientists during the past four decades is so overwhelming that one is inclined to agree with Sir John Hunt (now Lord Hunt) who said, "I believe in the yeti."

Notes and References

1. Richard Cavendish (ed.), *Encyclopaedia of the Unexplained.*
2. J.A. Jackson, *Abominable Snowman Adventure by Ralph Izzard*, London, 1955 *pp. 265-70* and *More than Mountains*, London, 1955. Cited in Harka Gurung, *Annapurna to Dhaulagiri.*
3. In Nepal, the 'yeti' has several synonyms such as Sukpa, Meete, Chute, Nyalmo, Rimi, Rakshi Bompo, Meito Kangmi (Tibetan name denoting 'filthy snowman'). One of the reports stated that a child born of a yeti mother and a Sherpa father was once discovered, in the sixties, at Chilunkha village in the Everest region.
4. 'New Light on Yeti Likely', *The Times of India*, 24 October 1975, p. 9.
5. *The Times of India*, 8 September 1964, editorial page.
6. A France-born surgeon, she spent two decades in her search for a creature called 'Almasty' in the Caucasus region.
7. *The Free Press Journal*, 11 March 1988, editorial page.
8. *The Times of India*, 25 May 1969, magazine section.
9. 'Snowman Seen in Siberia', *The Hindustan Times*, 5 February 1978.
10. 'She had a look at a "Snowman"'[2] *The Hindustan Times*, New Delhi, 20 May 1981.
11. *The Hindustan Times*, 17 September 1981.
12. More than 200 sightings were reported from the Hubei province in China in the course of four years ending 1980. AFP reported earlier, quoting a New China News Agency (NCNA) account, that a scientific expedition sent to Shenmongijia, a mountain in Hubei province, had gathered some traces of hair, excrements and footprints with the help

of the local population and cadres of the People's Liberation Army. Also see 'China's Version of the Abominable Snowman,' *The Statesman*, New Delhi, 25 October 1984 and Dennis Bloodworthk, 'The Abominable Chinese Snowman,' *The Times of India*, New Delhi, 28 September 1980.

13. 'Food Pinched by Hungry Snowman', *The Statesman*, 12 April 1992.

2

The Dark Secret of the Himalayas

Lord John Hunt, the leader of the first successful expedition to Everest, declared on his return from the mountain: "I believe in the yeti. I have seen his tracks, heard his yelping call, listened to the first-hand experiences of local people, similar to those you will read." He asks: "Indeed, why should he not exist? That they (The *Daily Mail* expedition 1954) did not sight a yeti is scarcely surprising. That evidence will be produced sooner or later, sufficient to convince the doubters beyond doubt."[1]

Sir John's Sherpa guida Tenzing Norgay had his roots in the Solu district in the foothills of Mount Everest. He was one of the firm believers in the yeti's existence. Amazingly enough, one of the leading non-believer's belonged to Russia, where field investigators discovered thousands of footprints, supposedly belonging to the abominable snowman. Vladimir Ratzec wrote in a book entitled, *The Riddle of Abominable Snowman*[2] that the creature called the yeti in Nepal was non-existent. According to him:

39

"The yeti may be found if we look for its remains and not for a living creature. The yeti may have existed but not now." He added: "Nothing is accidental in people's memory. Even fairy tales have some foundations for them. This is true of the snowman too. The vividness of legends about the yeti and similar creatures, told by Sherpas, Mongols, Tibetans and other central Asian peoples leaves no doubt that some basis must exist for them."

Hamish MacInnes, who has been credited with extensive travels on the Himalayas and Karakorums in the nineteen fifties, was also among those who refused to believe in the yeti's existence. "I am convinced that the yeti is alive only in the demon-filled minds of the Nepalese. But I do think that it was very much alive as recently as 500 years ago. I now stand in the ranks of unbelievers and that is after having travelled extensively throughout the Himalayas and Karakorums."[3] His version found no support from his trekking mate, Major Douglas, who thinks "there may be a yeti in the wild unfrequented valleys of Nepal or Tibet." MacInnes attributes the footprints he came across to the paws of a Himalayan brown bear. Its claws extend one-and-a-half to two inches beyond its paws, whereas the black bear's claws are shorter and curved, making it difficult sometimes to see their indentations in the snow. The impression often looks like toe marks without claws: "Some of the prints which I measured were four inches by twelve inches with a stride up to thirty-eight inches. These were of a black bear and as the hind paws superimpose on the forepaw spoor, it is often difficult to tell the difference between human and bear prints."

In the same article, MacInnes makes a passing reference to other rivals 'hunting for our big cousin' in the late nineteen fifties. "One party was rather cosmopolitan, consisting of Tom Slick, the Texan oil millionaire, and a shapely Californian heiress with several Britons and Celts for good measure. The other was the University of Leningrad expedition, whose camp-loving Pamir yeti at one time stole their pneumatic boat. On another occasion several of the expedition members saw a fur-clad figure high in the icy ranges of Pamir." He also makes a reference to the natives' talk in Kulu (Himachal Pradesh, India) of their rajah having brought a snow-woman and given her an honoured position among the royal wives. "The rajah was apparently well satisfied with his latest spouse but never once, no matter what he did, did he hear her speak...."[4]

It is indeed a challenging task to adduce evidence about the existence of a creature visible only at night (*Hominid nocturna*, as it has been termed by scientists) in the wild, desolate tracts untrod by human feet.

Where the treeline ends and the snowline begins, the very sight of tracks indented on the snow by giant-size human feet sends a shiver down the spine. If the monster had really passed that way, how was it surviving in that hostile habitat where nothing grows, save a stubble of moss on ice and stone and that too only during spring. Signs of fauna and flora begin to fade at that altitude. It is only after the thaw that the landscape comes alive on the intermediate sub-Alpine ranges lying between the eternal snow and vegetation zones. Even avian life, as spoken of by mountaineers, explorers and lepidopterists is a rarity for the better part of the year. In his book, *The Sherpa and the Snowman*, cited earlier, Stonor gives a graphic account of the fauna and flora that his party came across on the snow-covered ranges during autumn and winter in Solu and Longmoche districts at the foothills of Mt. Everest. The yak is indeed present there in herds. So are wild snow-crows and red and yellow-billed choughs. The snow bear is the only wild beast whose footprints can be confused with the abominable snowman's. The more baffling aspect of the chance discovery of footprints is the straight track that they cut single file across miles of snow expanse till they merge into the horizon, the vague sign to its obscure cave dwelling beyond the crystal white ranges.

Sightings At Makalu (1957-58)

News came thick and fast in the second half of the fifties about yeti sightings by mountaineering teams in the Nepal Himalayas. To mention just a few, during the 1957–58 climbing season, a French expedition was camping near Makalu. Its successful leader, P. Bordet and member, M. Latreille, had undertaken a geological survey of the Barun Valley (in the vicinity of Makalu and Mt. Everest.) They were accompanied by a Sherpa team. So far, this region had remained unexplored by any geologist. The expedition members completed the previous year's inconclusive geological survey of the Makalu area. They found footprints which looked barely a day-old on the Barun Pass near Makalu. These footprints were the size of a human being's and they had four toes. The survey team followed their trail for nearly a mile. They ascended the hard rock and ultimately disappeared among the cliffs. Members who photographed the footprints thought they belonged to some animal which always walked on its two legs like a man. They did not, however, see this animal in flesh.

Sightings Near Mt. Everest (1959-61)

The first Japanese yeti expedition sponsored jointly by Japanese Educational Television and Mainichi

Broadcasting System to the Everest region (1959–61) had only heard about the yeti. Its members could not actually see the creature. This expedition was headed by Teizo Ogawa (59), President, Japan Yeti Studies Group and professor in the Department of Anatomy, Medical Faculty, University of Tokyo.

Ogawa returned in February 1960 after a three-month stay in the Everest region. "We have returned convinced," he told the press at Kathmandu, "of the presence of an animal-like human being in the Himalayas which is more intelligent than the normal gorilla." He did not see any yeti or its footprint. Instead, he brought back ten specimens, including one piece of skin and a few bones, supposedly the yeti's, for close scientific examination.

Sightings At Ganesh Himal

Footprints of the mysterious creature came to the notice of the members of the Japanese Ganesh Himal (24,299 ft.) expedition in 1958 after its Sherpa members heard voices — sounding like *koo, koo, koo* — near their camp at night. The yeti peeped thrice into their camp. The team was headed by Y. Hotta. It had Mureyama as its manager and S. Takebushi, a journalist, as one of its members. The climbers discovered the yeti's footprints a few days later near a base camp set up at over 16,000 ft. (over 4800 m) altitude. They made drawings of the footprints and followed them for some distance before they disappeared under fresh snow.

The main topic of discussion among mountaineers returning to Kathmandu in 1958–59 was; 'Has any mountaineer seen it?' A minor yeti's footprints were noticed by the Keio University (Japan) team led by K. Kato at an altitude of 17,000 ft. (about 5120 m) on the Dhaulagiri range.

Sightings at Jugal Himal

The Japanese expedition that assaulted Jugal Himal, the British team to Annapurna, the Swiss climb over Dhaulagiri, the Indian party to Cho Oyu and the American snowman expedition to Barun Valley in the neighbourhood of the Everest and Makalu ranges were all asking each other if any mountaineers had seen the elusive creature. How come they never saw it and the Sherpas alone sighted it.'

Other Sightings

The Japanese team members stated: "We don't believe such a creature exists but our Sherpas do." The Swiss shared the negative view. P. J. Wallace, a district official from Nigeria working in the British Colonial Services, ruled out its existence but he would not disbelieve his Sherpas. Norman Dyhrenfurth asserted he had proof. He had photographed the hand of a dead yeti at Pangboche monastery and seen its scalp. He believed "the yeti is powerful, intelligent and strong".

Among the Sherpa climbers enjoying international repute, there were five who participated in that year's expeditions to Makalu and Manaslu (near Mt. Everest), Cho Oyu, Annapurna and Dhaulagiri. Norbu Lama and Dawa Tenzing denied having seen a yeti, though they expressed their firm faith in its existence. Dawa Temba, a trusted member of Dyhrenfurth's expedition (1958) claimed to have seen a yeti. As a member of the *Daily Mail* snowman expedition, Temba had seen, by torchlight, a four-foot tall yeti collecting frogs. He had served as a member of several Western expeditions. Early in May 1958, on his return from the mountains, he claimed at Kathmandu that he was the first and the only Sherpa till that time to have sighted a yeti in the upper Dudh Kosi valley. He was on duty as a night watchman

44

outside the climbers' camp occupied by Gerald Russell when he saw, by torchlight, a biped covered with hair. The yeti escaped before he could chase it.

A few of the climbers came very close to sighting the yeti in person. Giavano Spani, a representative of *Il Tempo* (journal) and the Italian Television, photographed, on a full-moon night, on 28 November 1959, a huge monkey-like creature at a 20,000 ft. (about 6060 m) altitude on the Dorje Lakpa range. His party comprising Sherpa hunters was asleep when they heard the sound of footsteps outside the cave where they had taken shelter. Spani went out and nearly 60 m away from the cave, located a huge monkey-like creature staring at him. It moved a few steps calmly but ran away as Spani shot the flash. The following morning Sherpa Nimondi found two very clear imprints of footsteps on the sand bank of a rivulet and shouted 'Yeti, yeti', since no other animal lived in the vicinity. No further trail could be located because of the ice and the stony surface. The Sherpas had come out of the cave only after the animal had disappeared.

In the Sixties

Next comes the testimony of Captain Tony Streather, who attempted Kanchenjunga, the world's third highest peak. A British climber, he had done successful climbing over Hindu Kush and Karakorum (Pakistan) ranges. He did not see any footprints but he firmly believed in the yeti's existence, although there was a lack of scientific data. "I believe there is some creature called the 'abominable snowman'." He denied that his team leader, Charles Evans, had said at Calcutta a few days earlier on return from the mountain, that the snowman did not exist in Himalayas. No sufficient proof of its existence was there nor was its exact shape known, was all that Evans had stated.

Alpinists were equally divided about the abominable snowman's existence. Canon Jules de Try, a Belgian ethonologist, who accompanied Raymond Lambert, the leader of the successful 1955 Franco-Swiss expedition to Langtang, said he made an extensive search for the yeti in Langtang valley but failed to find any. People of this valley believe that the snowman was in existence in the area. They said there were many caves on altitudes ranging from 16,000 ft. to 20,000 ft.. but they (the local people) failed to give the precise 'address' of any snowman seen in the recent past. Lambert too had denied having seen any such footprints.

Nepal's claim to being one of the probable homes of this mysterious primate cannot be lightly brushed aside as a myth. Several Western journalists, explorers and anthropologists have tried to collect evidence on the creature's personality, habitat, movement and lifestyle. Jean Ellis, a journalist, who visited Kathmandu in 1958, cites a 'knowledgeable abbot of a monastery' near Kathmandu, for the prevailing belief among the local Tibetan people that there exist three species of the Yeti.[5] Ellis's report said the different species vary in stature. The Nyalmo type grows to a 15 ft. height, is carnivorous, feeds on yak and mountain sheep, and moves about in groups led by a female of the species. A second type, called Rimi, which attains a height up to eight feet, is both carnivorous and a vegetarian and lives at altitudes between 8,000 and 10,000 feet. The third type, called Rakshi or Rakshi Bompo,. is barely five feet tall. This type is a vegetarian and steals grain and millets from outlying water mills and store huts.

Jeffrey McNeely, the joint leader of the Arun Valley Wild Life Expedition, said in a report he sent to the Nepalese Foreign Ministry that his team members Edward Cronin and Edward Emery had found strange tracks outside their tent. Each footprint in these tracks was 22 cm long and 12 cm wide, with a well-rounded heel: "The big toe was the largest, somewhat lower on the foot than the other four toes."

McNeely further stated that his party had seen a distinct line of prints and details of track.... The tracks did not even remotely resemble those of a bear or snow leopard. They seemed to be tracks of a primate, and monkeys (both langurs and macaques) have been seen in the area". "The footprints are", McNeely continued, "considerably larger than those of any monkey and are much wider in relation to the length than are tracks of monkeys".

Ashkenazi also gives an account of the circumstances under which he had sighted, from the rear, an exceptionally tall tribal near the railway station yard at Peshawar way back in the thirties. (See also Appendix 1.)

Ashkenazi, who claims he is one who had 'personally encountered' the yeti in the Himalayas and reared a she-yeti baby way back in 1938, makes a passing reference in his accounts to the skeletal hand of a yeti preserved in Pangboche monastery in the neighbourhood of Everest. He points out the resemblance that he noticed between its elongated phalanges and metacarpus with that of the child yeti he had reared before its premature death. Ashkenazi claims that he "personally encountered" the yeti in the Sonamarg region of the Kashmir Valley. After a tourist, named Alison Isabel MacDonald, was reported missing, in a letter to *The Hindustan Times* editor, Ashkenazi wrote that he could help find the girl, 'most probably' kidnapped by a yeti, and also locate its cave with the help of leylines.[6] According to Ashkenazi: "Leylines are imperceptible to human senses and are followed by the yetis who are highly psychic. The

47

underground caves where they conceal their prey are usually at the intersection of these leylines which follow the hidden courses of underground waterways. I located a pair of yetis by following such leylines as recently as 21 June 1981 in the Pir Panjal above Gulmarg, Kashmir." He submitted a report along with photographs to the Jammu and Kashmir Government. He further wrote: "I have in the past also reared a baby female yeti in the Himalayas. She is now dead."

The yeti's personality, as emerging from Ashkenazi's account, leaves the impression that the *jangli aadmi* (wild man) whom he had sighted at Peshawar was a survivor of the Stone Age when mankind had yet to develop coherence in speech and learn how to clothe himself. He does not call him the 'abominable snowman' though he asserts that there was a "striking similarity between the gigantic ten-feet-tall Sasquatch (yeti of British Columbia, whom the Lillocet Indians call *Hailo haux* or *Hailo laux*) and the equally tall Negroid yeti found in the north-western Himalayas whom the Afghans and Pathans and other tribals of Pakistan's North West Frontier call *Hailo log* (literally the black, hairy people) to this day." (See Appendices 1 and 2.)

Ashkenazi cites too the prevailing belief among top anthropologists and scientists that Sasquatch of Canada and Bigfoot of North America migrated in prehistoric times from China and Central Asia to the north-west of Canada via Bering Strait.

Voices in the Dark
Should the foregoing observations not be enough, one has to recall the mysterious voices heard in 1987 in several hamlets of Kashmir. A survey team of the Jammu and Kashmir State Wild Life Department reported the sighting of a hairy figure at night, which called persons

by name and asked a medical officer posted at Baramula to send medicine supplies. A United News of India (UNI) report carried by Indian dailies said one Riaz Qazi, a forest ecologist, led his team to several hamlets around the Kangan block of Srinagar district. Here people told the team members that they had occasionally noticed a hairy figure disappearing into the snow. Zaman Mohammed Khan, a watchman at a sheep farm at Barbul village, told the survey team that he had heard a mysterious voice on the night of 14 January 1987, calling names of people employed on the farm.

On 16 January he again heard similar cries throughout the night. Khan went out with two of his colleagues to investigate and saw a hairy figure, three to four feet tall. It walked some distance and vanished. Two other persons in the vicinity, Dr. Balwant Singh posted at Baramula village, and Mohammed Dandli, who was in-charge of the *hamam* (bathing place) attached to the mosque, told the Wild Life Department official that on 14 January they heard similar voices at night.[7]

Three Species of Yeti

Three distinct types of yeti are believed to exist in Sikkim. Going by their size they are called miegye, Demi and Chudey or Chudeh. A part of the belief in the existence of these creatures is derived from the Tibetans who call them Dzu Teh and Mihteh. They probably migrated to Tibet from neighbouring Nepal. Miegye, or the superhuman, is regarded a demigod, twelve feet tall, a ferocious carnivore dwelling at high altitudes. The second type, having a medium-size stature, is also a carnivore. The smallest and the least offensive, a dweller of the valleys is called Chudey. Punyabajra Lama also speaks of a similar classification. (See Appendix 5).

In 1978 when the Sikkim Forest Department launched a project to trap or photograph a yeti, Ara Singh, a departmental official, had actually run across a yeti nearly four-and-a-half feet in height. Gangtok-based correspondents of *The Times of India* and *Indian Express* cited unconfirmed reports of a giant-size yeti having tossed a yak 200 to 500 yards away! There was no mark of dragging at the 15,000 ft. (about 4550 m) high Kishong La. Sightings of the yeti were also reported from the Kesey Dombong tract in Lachung valley. The tract selected for photography stretched from Zemee to Dzongiri; however, it yielded no trace.

Though disbelief in the yeti's existence was noticed to be receding by the turn of the sixties, even highly financed and well-equipped American, Japanese and multinational expeditions to the Nepal Himalayas had failed to locate a living specimen of the aforementioned three species. No doubt, such expeditions returned only the richer, as a result of an accumulation of yarns about the yeti spun out by Sherpas or peripatetic Tibetans arriving across the border in Nepal.

Tracks in Russia

What contributed to the growing belief in the continuing existence of the Stone Age survivor was the field investigation undertaken in the former USSR by a few scientific bodies. Early in the sixties, *Kosmolskaya Gazeta* (a Soviet youth newspaper) reported Nina Grinyeva's version of the findings of a 1979 expedition led by Igor Tatsl. A member of an amateur team, searching for the snowman in the Pamir Ala mountain in Tadzikstan, Grinyeva narrates in the journal how she came across a mysterious creature near a river bank. It had a "massive frame, almost rectangular with a very thin neck". The creature had stopped and she saw its arms hanging loosely by its sides. When she approached, it looked at her "piercingly but without malice", turned and went away.[8]

Another team member, Gelian Siforova, claimed that she saw a creature "about two metres thirty centimetres (about seven feet seven inches) tall with a powerful frame" seated on a lake-side rock. Igor Tatsl observed that many members of his team had overcome earlier scepticism after finding giant footprints and interviewing local shepherds who had encountered a hairy, human-like creature.

Igor Kozlov, a member of the USSR Geographical Society, based his findings on fifty photographs and plaster casts that led him to believe that the mysterious creature preferred high forests to snow zones. A veteran of high mountain expeditions, Kozlov wrote in the journal *Socialist Industry*[9] that the snowman reported from the Caucasus mountains between the Baltic and Caspian Sea and Tyan Shan mountains on the China border in Central Asia moves at about twelve kmph and its feet are structured for rapid movement over stony ground. To protect itself against rains it lives in shelters whose floor is covered with the litter of tree branches and leaves. An unsocial type, apparently this creature is a loner, sleeping by day and leaving its shelter at dusk in search of food. Possibly, it is a distant cousin of the Neanderthal man. From the fact that this creature turned aggressive only in five instances out of a total of 5000 encounters, cited by those who claimed to have seen the creature, one inferred that it was not dangerous to human beings. No evidence was available on this creature's mating habits.

The Russian creatures may not be living or moving in flocks, though one account from the north-eastern Himalayas credited them with holding group dances at night, while Punyabajra Lama (see Appendix 5) said that its flocks were led by a female of the species.

In the Russian context, the most reliable evidence was attributed to Jeanne Koffman, a disciple of Professor Boris Porshnev (a historian). She noted that in the northern Caucasus the creature was sighted by Ruslan Shamanov, a sports inspector, from his night lodge. The creature that he sighted in the dark did not exceed ordinary human height, though sometimes it appeared to be taller. It had a stooping posture, a squat head resting squarely on its shoulders, a sloping forehead, long arms and fingers and a red face.[10]

Koffman's findings affirm that the dimensions of the creature's foot were: 25.5 cm in length, 12 to 13 cm in width; and 1.5 to 2 cm in depth. Its stride measured 120 to 130 cm and it left a track in a straight line.

Persons who had claimed to have sighted this creature (they included local village level officials) stated the creature was 2 metres (6'6") tall and wore deerskin. It belonged to a primitive tribe that flees at the sight of hunters. The creature whistles, lives on raw meat and Taiga shrubs and sometimes steals food from village homes. It probably belongs to a tribe that fled at the advance of more developed tribes. In Siberia this creature was known as Chuchuna and in Caucasus as 'Almasty' or 'Almos'.[11]

The Missing Link?

It was the Russian Professor Boris Porshnev's belief that the abominable snowman could possibly be a survivor of Neanderthal man. It is possible the yeti of the Himalayas is a larger anthropoid forming the link between ape and man. A Soviet hydrologist, A.G. Pronin, saw twice an anthropoid near the Fedchenko glacier. Also, Prince Peter of Greece had reported the actual capture of an abominable snowman in Sikkim. Porshnev, Pronin and the Greek Prince Peter were eminent predecessors of Jeanne Koffman.

Eyewitness Accounts from the USA

Hundreds of eyewitness accounts have been reported with respect to the 'Bigfoot' from the USA[12], where one could least expect to find it amidst intensive industrialisation and urbanisation. Several eyewitnesses have described this creature. According to Charles C. Edmonds, it is a giant, ten feet tall. It had left tracks on sand, soil, mud and even on snow near lakes, rivers and mountains. Surprisingly, one of the species had left tracks on the bank of river Lewis in such an intensely urbanised state as Washington. Casts of the tracks were made by observers and sent for examination to zoologists, anthropologists and naturalists. A doctor, specialising in the study of feet (and the head of the Crime Laboratory, Portsmouth, Oregon), dismissed the evidence as of 'no consequence in identifying the Bigfoot'. The weight of the creature was estimated at 800lb. From the river side it had emerged dripping and the footmarks indicated tracks of the creature crossing the bank and returning to the river. The footprints measured 18 inches in length and 8 inches across the ball of the foot, almost twice the size of a human being's. Eyewitnesses described it as a hairy giant endowed with enormous strength and cunning.

The writer of this account added that there exist hundreds of eyewitness reports of actual sighting. Of the three specific instances, one version had it that the Bigfoot began peering through the glass panes of a house, sending its solitary female occupant into shrieks. On two occasions, men were carried away by the Bigfoot into the woods. In a fourth case, the monster had tried to gain entry into a house by turning its latch. It was only when the occupant threatened to pull out his gun that the creature left. The writer points out that many anthropoid creatures appear to be in existence, although unseen, in different parts of the USA.

According to some observers, the Bigfoot has enormous feet with large, strong toes adapted for climbing and for achieving swimming proficiency. Its arms are unusually long, hanging loose from the shoulders down to the knees. The Bigfoot normally walks with a stoop.

The face colouring of the Bigfoot ranges from concrete to a dense black. It has small eyes and earlobes, sticking rather close to the sides of the head. The nostrils are usually dilated and lips almost non-existent on an abnormally large mouth. The colour of the hair could be white, tan, brown, silver, grey and even black. The most striking feature of Bigfoot is its extremely foul stink. It emits sounds that are 'difficult to be classified into anything known'.

American scientists are still far too puzzled about the exact classification of this creature. They suggest more objective investigation and research to establish its true identity.

Distribution across Different Continents

The *Encyclopaedia of the Unexplained* carries a world map depicting the abominable snowman's distribution across different continents in both hemispheres. This volume also reproduces a photograph of huge footprints taken near Annapurna (Nepal) by Don Whillans, deputy leader of the British expedition to this mountain's south face in 1970. The toe marks of the creature's giant sole are distinct; the stride spans unusually large; and the track, visible for miles, is remarkably straight. Both Whillans and his teammate, Doug Houston, saw (through a telescope) a two-legged creature disappearing behind trees in a distant mountain. It could not be a hallucination since Houston was earlier an unbeliever in the existence of the yeti.

The *Encyclopaedia* entry just cited also mentions that the Swedish botanist and naturalist Carl Linnaeus, described the snowman as a 'creature resembling man' and also as *Homo nocturnas*, (the 'man of the night'), rarely encountered. The *Encyclopaedia*, also refers to the latest field researches of Jeanne Koffman in the Caucasus preceded by Boris Porshnev, and J.R. Rinchen of Mongolia.

According to the brief entry in the *Encyclopaedia*, this half-human creature called Almos was sighted in the nineteenth century by a Russian (Colonel Nikolai Prsvalsky) during his exploration 'deep into Mongolia and Gobi desert'. Further scientific investigation was not permitted by the Imperial Court of China, apparently because the discovery of a half-human would prove embarrassing.

Another synonym for Almos in Russia is *Snezhnyy Cuelovck* (meaning snowman). In the non-Russian-speaking States, it is called *Ahananyu* (forest man), *Bianbanguli* (in Azerbaijan), *Dev* (in Pamir region) and *Kiik Adam* (wild man) in Kazakhistan.

A Profile of the Yeti

The yeti's shadowy visage has been described in diverse ways by different persons who claimed to have glimpsed this creature before it 'vanished' behind the forest cover. Almost all sightings of footprints make emphatic reference to the toe turned backward and the remaining four toes webbed together as in a claw. According to many observers, the arms hang loose from the shoulders,

55

reaching almost up to the knees. If a she-yeti, the creature runs across the snowscape with breasts swept back over either shoulder. But for the yeti's face, which is hairless, the entire body is covered by black, brown or reddish fur one-and-a-half to two centimetres thick, skirting the waist with a thick undergrowth. The eyes are 'soulless', according to one version which describes the American species.

The large-size Himalayan yeti is credited with a head rising conically upward from a broad jaw over a protruding chin. Lips are almost missing, while the nostrils below a broad nose are unusually dilated. The earlobes are sticking along either side of the temple. The unusually large head rests, through a short neck, on broad, square shoulders. While the arms (hanging loose from the shoulders) are unusually long, the legs are disproportionately short compared to the entire body.

The most obnoxious part of the yeti's presence is its extremely foul stink which few can endure.

The Need for Further Research

Explorers, anthropologists, zoologists and naturalists have been engaged for almost a century now in the quest of a creature who may provide a clue to the mystery of the missing link. This creature may be the rarest among the survivors of a species of half-humans, half-apes, fast getting extinct. Every sighting of the footprints is followed, as the *Encyclopaedia of the Unexplained* remarks, "by a deathly hush". Yet, every sighting has only added to information about the creature which cannot be mistaken for a Himalayan bear or an oversized ape. This unique creature can see in the dark and it can sniff human presence from long distances.

Climbers in Nepal have heard, at night, the yeti's shrieks and eerie whistles coming down wind, while natives claim it yelps, mutters, mews and bleats. Accounts available from the Nepal Himalayas are not wholly imaginary.

Indeed, today, further detailed field investigation is called for to relieve public curiosity about the mysterious creature, whether abominable or adorable. Mass communication media owe a duty to lift the veil of secrecy over everything under the sun. The earth's secrets have seemingly got exhausted and human beings have crossed several frontiers of space to explore the planets and other regions of the universe. Even then there is one secret still left shrouded in a shadow. Hence, voluntary organisations like the media of more advanced nations like Japan, the USA or the UK, which plan to undertake the discovery of the last secret about the ancestry of man deserve financial support from the government and other financial institutions.

With the recent tremendous advances in science and technology, probably, scientists could consider the use of sophisticated satellite photography to track down and capture on film the yeti and its lifestyle.

And now over to Madan Mohan Gupta who made a solo effort to gather first-person accounts of certain rare encounters with the yeti in the Nepal Himalayas.

Notes and References

1. Charles Stonor, *The Sherpa and the Snowman*, Foreword.
2. Vladimir Ratzec, *The Riddle of the Abominable Snowman*.
3. Quoted from 'The Abominable Myth', Burmah Shell News, Vol. VIII, No.1, January 1959, pp. 12-13.
4. *Ibid.*
5. Ellis's report was published by the London-based *Sunday Dispatch*, and cited by Brian S. N. Ashkenazi in *The Indian Express* (Sunday edition), 2 February 1981.

6. *The Hindustan Times,* 17 September 1981, Letters to the Editor.
7. 'Strange Voices Revive Mystery of Yeti', UNI report, *The Statesman,* 24 January 1987.
8. 'She Had a Look at the Snowman' (Reuters) reported in *The Hindustan Times,* 20 May 1981.
9. Reproduced as 'The Snowman Is Not Really Abominable', *The Statesman,* 12 December 1984.
10 'Snowman: Renewed Interest in USSR', *The Times of India,* 16 May 1978.
11. 'Yeti-like Creature Sighted in Siberia', *The Times of India,* 6 February 1978.
12. Charles C. Edmonds, 'Is There an American Yeti?' *The Times of India;* 25 May 1969, p. iii of the weekly magazine.

Part II

Individual Testimonies
(Gathered by Madan M. Gupta
between 1957 and 1968)

3
A Close Brush with the Yeti
(as told by Yogi Narahari Nath)

What looked like a giant of a man stalked past me within the twinkling of an eye as I was still gasping on a snow-bound range below Ganesh Himal. Almost eight feet tall, he stood on a pair of legs that appeared much smaller compared to his abnormally long arms dangling, shoulders downward, to his knees. One single stride that he took could easily cover four steps of my own.

While we (my guide and myself) were panting at every step of our climb at that altitude, he flit past me almost effortlessly within a trice. He seemed to take no notice of us as he bounded off, even though we were barely five feet apart. His entire body was covered with a coat of thick long hair, both dark and grey.

I was taken by surprise over the creature's enormous physique and his weird features. For a person stalking nude on the perennial snowland, he seemed endowed with extraordinary endurance born of natural acclimatisation.

I glanced back at my guide, a Bhotia*, to ask him to throw some light on the astonishing creature we had

*Bhotias are people living on the Nepal—Tibet border. They make a living sometimes by working as high altitude porters for foreign climbers.

just seen. To my utter surprise, I found that my Tibetan Sherpa guide had swooned on the hard snow floor while the yak carrying the load of my baggage was missing. I asked the guide, when he came around in response to my vigorous shaking, if he could tell me where our yak had vanished? Still trembling, the guide pointed towards a crevasse where the yak was standing. I took out a camera from rucksack and sprinted in the direction in which strange creature had gone. By that time the monster had covered a long distance. I could now see him climbing a steep rock about 500 yards away. I took a few photographs quickly before the creature vanished behind the fog-wrapped rocks. I was still busy clicking when my guide came rushing to caution me: "Don't photograph him," the guide pleaded, still shivering with fear. "He is one of the dieties from the Himalaya. If he came to know that you were photographing him, he would return and kill us." Unfortunately, the photograph I got was all blurred due to dense fog on the snowscape.

What I could gather from my Tibetan guide was that this monster was held in veneration by Tibetans, who called him a yeti. He rarely crossed a man's path. It was the first occasion in his entire life that the 55-year-old Tibetan Sherpa actually saw a yeti though he had heard legends about it all his life. His elders had told him that one must lie down as soon as one sights a yeti since the prevalent belief was that he (yeti) would not touch the dead though he carried away living human beings. The guide could not conceal his dismay over the fact that the yeti had spared us though I stood barely five feet from the path taken by him. He attributed my survival to the fact of my being an ochre-robed sadhu whom the yetis regarded as venerable.

This is how the noted Sanskrit scholar, Yogi Narahari Nath narrated his personal experience. When he sighted the yeti, he was on a pilgrimage from Nepal to Mount Kailash in Tibet (in 1050). The Yogi said it was the first time that he came to know about the existence of the yeti. Though he undertook several treks in snow-bound tracts of the Nepal Himalayas in subsequent years, such an encounter was never repeated. Indeed, he had heard many a fascinating tale about the yeti. In the Yogi's opinion, the yeti was a reality though it was sighted only rarely. An anthropologist himself, the Yogi fondly hoped that one day the yeti would come into full view to the great benefit of the wider field of science.

In Narahari Nath's opinion, the word 'Yeti' has been derived from its Sanskrit original, 'Yaksha'. This word occurs all too frequently in almost the entire Sanskrit literature on the Himalayas. The 'Yaksha' is described as a person of superhuman stature having a coat of thick hair all over his body excluding the face. Half-human, half-beast, he is credited with both wild nature and intelligence. High altitudes in the Himalayas are cited as his native home. One comes across a mention of the Yaksha in literature wherever the tribes and beasts of Himalayas are mentioned. He dwells, according to these accounts, in isolated and inaccessible mountains far away from human settlements. People living in the Himalayas regard the yeti as attendants of gods and prefer to avoid their company out of superstitious beliefs.

The Yogi pointed out that the 'Yaksha' remains untraceable today. Nobody had seen him in person. To the Yogi, it did not sound very logical to assume that the Yaksha was a mere figment of human imagination and the yeti a myth. When the rest of the Himalayan tribes and creatures cited in Sanskrit literature have survived, it would be a little illogical to argue that the

Yaksha is a myth. The Sanskrit description of a Yaksha bears a striking resemblance to the popular notion about his physique or to accounts of those claiming to have glimpsed the creature. It is possible that this monster, a link between ape and man, may not be almost extinct and the survivors of the species may be numerically too few in the Nepal Himalayas to be easily sighted by explorers. Those still surviving prefer to lead a sequestered life in their hideouts. That was one reason why they managed to elude all search by those who trekked on the Himalayas.

During his long treks in the Himalayas, the Yogi felt convinced that the Yaksha cited in the ancient Sanskrit literature was none else than the modern yeti. Yogis meditating in Himalaya have given accounts of yetis resembling those found in Sanskrit literature. A cave-dweller, the yeti is both carnivorous and vegetarian. With a dense overgrowth of hair all over his body, he is endowed with superhuman size and prowess.

Each fully developed yeti can easily match the strength of a wrestler. His lung power, stamina and endurance are at least ten times those of an average human being's. He is a swift climber on rocky mountains.

The Yogi said it was quite probable that the lost tribe of Yaksha had now come to acquire its current name, yeti, synonymous with other Tibetan variants.

Ancient Sanskrit literature carries allusions to four tribes — Nag, Kinner, Gandharva and Yaksha — among the inhabitants of the Himalayas. While Nag, Kinner and Gandharva were described as those leading an organised village life, the Yaksha was endowed with the innate power of quick disappearance. The other three tribes were still inhabiting the Himalayas. So, the Yogi argued, there is reason to believe that the Yaksha (or the yeti) is not an imaginary creature.

4

Abducted into a Yeti's Cave

Kuisang, a 50-year-old woman, was engaged as a domestic servant by a Tibetan friend of mine living at Kathmandu. I had known her for nearly ten years as a soft-spoken woman of few words. Her dark hair parted in the middle fell gently over her shoulders as she flit about in her colourful *srong* on festive days. She hailed from Tarke, a village near Helmu, five days' trek north of Kathmandu. She belonged to the Sherpa Tamang tribe. My friend's family also hailed from the neighbourhood of Tarke.

Kuisang fully remembered how her elder sister, then about eight years old, had suddenly disappeared while playing with a group of children that included herself and reappeared quite as dramatically six years later. The story of her disappearance and return was common knowledge in the neighbourhood.

Kuisang says she had a sister named U-lee two years older than herself. Tarke is situated on a mountain range rising roughly to an 8,000-foot altitude. One afternoon, both sisters joined another group of girls of their age in playing with pebbles outside the village.

"We were playing," she began, "at the end of a turning at the rear of a big rock. The wind here was gentler and warmer and the place concealed from the villagers' view."

"After a few rounds of the game, my sister U-lee asked me to wait till she collected better pebbles from the other side of the rock. When she did not return, we thought she had taken a pretty long time in collecting pebbles. At first we shouted her name loud. Later, we ran around to search her out, calling her back all the time. To our utter surprise, there was no trace of U-lee. We felt scared by her mysterious disappearance amid the wilderness of the mountain range."

Kuisang continued: "We returned home to inform our people of her disappearance. My parents immediately sent out a search party, fearing that she had been attacked by a bear or some other wild beast. The party searched the entire neighbourhood till sunset. The search was resumed the following morning without yielding any result. U-lee was now given up as lost. Had she been devoured by some beast? If so, there should have been some trace of my missing sister's clothes."

"As the years passed, our family and the village people lost all hope of U-lee's return. My mother would often weep over the loss of her first-born and I missed U-lee, be it at work or play. The village people developed a fright for the place where we had played our last game with U-lee."

"Parents forbade the kids to go behind the large rock, their favourite playground. The prejudice did not last long. There being no better playground, children again started reassembling there for play."

Kuisang recalled that Tarke did not have a school worth the name. In a *ghyang* (lamasery) in the neighbourhood, an aged lama used to teach alphabets to

66

boys. The girls stayed back at home, helping mothers in domestic chores or fetching water in buckets from the neighbourhood waterfall. Our mornings were always frosty as the village was situated high on the mountain. The village people used to have an early lunch around ten o'clock. If the day was clear and snow-free, children would gather in bright sunshine on their playground.

One afternoon, six years after U-lee had vanished, one of our playmates, a boy, suddenly raised an alarm and ran towards the village, having sighted something very frightening. All of us rushed towards the village, scared of some grave danger.

The boy was nervous and trembling. He pointed towards the mountain, saying that he had seen a large, hairy creature carrying another like him. The other hairy creature that he had unloaded was still lying on the spot where it was abandoned.

Alarmed, nearly a dozen villagers collected whatever weapons they could seize in a hurry and rushed towards the danger spot. Children were warned to stay indoors. I peeped from a chink in the door of my house and observed ten minutes later that the village people were now returning. The man at the head was carrying in his arms a human being. They were highly agitated and engaged in making wild guesswork about the creature in their possession. It occurred to me that they had captured a yeti alive. After a few minutes, a number of men came forward to our home to call my mother. Nervous as I was, I rushed to the place where the creature sat surrounded by people.

What we saw was a human being, a hideous girl in the nude emitting a foul stench. She looked extremely weak and emaciated. Her filthy hair was matted into locks. Everyone gave her a pathetic look. I stooped a little to get a clearer view and was dumbfounded. The girl was none else than U-lee, my sister who had disappeared six years back! I wanted to confirm my first impression before recognising her. I spoke aloud, "U-lee", and the 'creature' responded, "Kuisang".

I was now certain that she was my sister. I jumped out to embrace her but people cautioned me. Others in the crowd also recognised her. The mystery was resolved when my mother came forward and accepted that she was her elder daughter. U-lee was so weak that she could not move and had to be carried in [my mother's] arms to our home.

We wrapped her in warm clothes. For the next three or four days, she wouldn't utter a single word. Already weak, she developed a fever too. Mother gave her *sampa* (barley powder) in a small quantity thrice a day followed by salted tea with butter several times. This helped her recover quickly. Almost a week later, mother washed her hair, gave her a hot water bath, snipped her nails, massaged her body with butter and gave her a proper dress before leaving her out for a sunbath.

As she felt at home, U-lee recalled how she was abducted. Before she disappeared, she said she was selecting a few pebbles in the stream running below the turning on the bridle path. Suddenly, a very heavy creature pounced upon her and lifted her body on its shoulder. She feared she had been attacked by some big bear and lost her senses.

As she came round later, she went on, she found herself lying on a large rock. A huge, hideous creature having a human face and a beast's body, covered with long tousled hair, was constantly staring at her. Once again, he lifted her bodily and resumed his big strides towards the snowy wilderness. She wept, cried aloud and beat her chest with her hands but to no avail. The beast went on almost for an hour and finally halted in a cave. The place was dark and stinking. The beast sat guard all night.

U-lee too could not sleep. She feared the moment she winked, she would be devoured. At daybreak, the creature went out, leaving her alone in the cave. She dared not stir out fearing the monster might be lurking somewhere. She would be caught and killed if she tried to escape.

The beast returned an hour later, bringing in its bare hands a few living snowfrogs and wild fruit. U-lee said she could not eat these things. She was extremely hungry and wanted something to eat. She tried fruits but they tasted bitter and were hardly enough to fill her belly. She cried aloud for food and freedom. The monster went out again and returned this time with some live fish. U-lee found raw fish better than wild fruit and ate the entire supply.

To begin with, U-lee said she had to survive on raw fish brought by the monster. Gradually, she began eating wild fruit and live frogs. The monster would not leave her alone for a long spell. As a result, U-lee had to compromise with her bondage and become the creature's consort. Later, he began to carry her out to the stream where she herself collected fish and frogs that she ate raw. As time elapsed, the creature was noticed to be behaving well. She was no more scared of him and began to behave like a partner of the creature who was, as she now realised, a yeti.

Her yeti did not like other yetis trying to befriend her. On several occasions, she witnessed fierce fights between her yeti and the others who tried to accost her.

The advent of her first winter with the yeti brought in its wake new problems for her survival. The mountain around was now covered with a thick layer of snow. The yeti hunted down a snow bear and both of them joined hands in skinning it. The bearskin kept her warm during the winter.

Following a snowfall, the river and all the trees were covered with a white blanket of ice. [Consequently], "no fruit, no frog, no fish". U-lee and her yeti had to trek long distances to descend to the vegetation line in search of food. On such occasions, U-lee suspected she was very near her village home. She wished she could run away to her parents but as ill-luck would have it, she was not familiar with the track leading to her village. Nor was her yeti ever off-guard about her movements. He would not allow her to walk out of sight.

U-lee spent five winters with the yeti. A sixth successive winter was at hand. Already, by this time, she had acquired two yak skins and three bearskins that fortified her against the coming winter. But one day she developed high fever, probably as a result of exposure to incessant snowfall. When it did not subside for several weeks, the monster carried her aloft and abandoned her on a rock near her village.

5

Ma-Yu's Escape from a Yeti

In the Rolwaling range [at places reaching up to 23,500 feet (7121 m)] of the Nepal Himalayas lies a slumbering village consisting of eleven homes at an altitude of nearly 9500 feet. Known locally as Thak, this village is inhabited mainly by Sherpas, famed for their prowess, endurance and stamina in mountain climbing. Towards one end of this mountain village stood the home of a couple, Thakin and Ma-Yu. The husband ran a watermill, almost three miles below the village. Thakin usually returned home after dark. When he was away, Ma-Yu would cleanse wool, spin yarn and weave carpets of various colours and designs. These fetched her a fancy price at the annual fair held at Beding, nearly eight days' trek from Thak. In the afternoon, this young Sherpa housewife loved to trek down to the watermill and return home with her husband, collecting fuelwood on the way.

A storm overtook them one evening while they were still slogging back home. It raged fairly long, forcing the couple to take shelter behind a big boulder. Once the storm subsided, it began to snow heavily. Thakin and

Ma-Yu lost their way, got separated and kept groping for hours. As it grew cold, they could walk no further and collapsed senseless due to excessive cold and exhaustion.

Next morning, after the snowfall was over, the village people went out to search for their sheep. They found Thakin lying cold and unconscious and brought him back to the village. There was no trace of his wife.

When Ma-Yu opened her eyes, as she was to recall many months later, she found herself in a stinking cave. A huge, woolly-haired, man-like creature with a ghoulish look sat staring at her. She could not guess who he could be and shut her eyelids out of fright. She began silently to recite a prayer that her mother had taught her to overcome fear and evil spirits. The creature now began licking her body. This gave her warmth. It rubbed the soles of her feet and was apparently trying to revive her senses. During the short, uneasy spell, Ma-Yu recalled the yeti tales she had heard and she now feared that she was in the clutches of a yeti. Her fear was to come true.

She had heard from village folk that the yeti kills human beings of their own sex but adores those of the opposite sex. She shuddered at the idea of having conjugal relations a second time in her life and that too with an ugly monster.

The yeti persisted with his efforts to warm up her body by covering it with his hairy limbs or by licking her body. Ma-Yu responded to this first aid. As soon as she opened her eyes, the creature yelled with delight and rushed out of the cave. It did not forget to block the mouth of the cave with a boulder.

In the haze hanging within the cave, she saw heaps of bones of different animals, dried-up shrubs and branches, possibly the remnants of the yeti's former meals. A foul stink of decaying flesh hung in the cave. She feared another attack on her nerves if she did not get a whiff of fresh air. She pulled herself up to the mouth of cave, peeped out through the chink on its closed exit and filled her nostrils with fresh air. Looking out through the chink, she found that ten feet ahead lay a deep gorge and she was confined to a cave on the top of a cliff. She now felt certain that it would be impossible for her to leap across the wide and deep gorge. She shuddered to think she would never be able to escape from her captor.

All this while, Thakin was not sitting idle. He went out to neighbouring villages in search of his missing wife. He felt certain that she had been rescued like him by someone who was probably keeping her as a hostage tempted by her beauty. A few others in the village were afraid that she might have been a victim of abduction by a yeti who was on the prowl in their neighbourhood. Though none had sighted it, they felt it definitely existed. They considered the yeti a cannibal and feared that by now Ma-Yu might have been devoured by her captor. Other were hopeful about her survival in the belief that male yetis did not kill women.

Ma-Yu remained untraced for another six months. One afternoon, Thakin sat tired and exhausted on the bank of a rivulet to catch a few fish for his meal. Suddenly, he saw a shaggy human being with a dirty face descending slowly down the cliff. As the human being cast off its woollen covering to wash her face and hands, Thakin discovered that it was none else than his missing wife. He leapt out of his hiding place behind the big boulder and rushed to Ma-Yu. She felt drawn by his footsteps and looked up in dismay. For the first time in the past six months, her eyes met her husband's and both were soon firmly clasping each other.

Ma-Yu now narrated to her husband the entire story of her captivity. She cautioned him against the cannibal, now expected any moment. She asked him to meet her every midday at the same place. She also entreated Thakin to bring along some *sampa* which she had not eaten for several months past. Ma-Yu reassured her husband that she would shortly unfold to him some plan for escape from the horrible goblin's clutches.

Several plans for escape were devised and discussed between husband and wife during their secret meetings in the next few days. Eventually, Ma-Yu hit upon a plan. "Get me a pair of big boots", she asked Thakin. It took the husband four days to get a pair ready. He delivered it to Ma-Yu along with a bag containing five pounds of maize flour. Ma-Yu now asked him to go back home and await her return which might be possible within the next six or seven days.

Back at the cave, Ma-Yu showed the yeti the bag of maize flour she had found lying along the rivulet where she had gone for fishing. She assured the yeti that *sampa* had a delicious taste. He liked it so much that he did not go out hunting till Ma-Yu's meagre stock ran out.

Ma-Yu now threatened to go on fast till the yeti brought more of *sampa* for her. He too wanted to have it. He asked her the source from which he could procure it. She was waiting for this query. She told him how he could reach the watermill on the far end of the village and find some *sampa* supply.

Ma-Yu was familiar with the villagers usual practice of leaving their maize in the evening in the bag attached to the watermill. It would be ground overnight into a fine powder. She prodded the yeti to visit the watermill early one morning. It did as it was told and stole the maize flour. It repeated these pilfering errands while the village lay asleep and regularly brought back sufficient supply. He had by now developed such a strong taste for the stolen maize flour that he stopped going out for hunting.

The next time when Ma-Yu met her husband he looked worried. He complained to her that *sampa* bags were being stolen from his watermill. Ma-Yu told him the secret behind their disappearance. She told him that she would advise the yeti to make use of the pair of big boots next time he went out to steal the flour bag. She reassured Thakin that she would be free within the next three days.

When the *sampa* stock in the cave thinned down the next time, the yeti decided to visit the watermill the following dawn. Ma-Yu advised him to use the pair of boots while returning to the cave. She gave him tips for putting on the boots. He did not like the idea, though he took the pair along.

Reaching the watermill, this time the yeti found a bag much heavier than any he had stolen so far. Even with his superhuman strength, he must have found it rather heavy to carry. He dragged the bag on the hard, stony surface for some distance with the boots still in one hand. Later, he took the bag as a backload and put on the boots. No sooner than he tried to climb a vertical cliff after clutching a big boulder than his boots slipped off the rock which he wanted to leap over. The huge boulder must have come hurtling down, burying the yeti under its weight. His tragic end came to Ma-Yu's notice shortly after sunrise. She lost no time in rejoining her husband.

6

"I became a Yeti's Wife"

Namche-Bazar, a bustling Sherpa village consisting of nearly 200 dwellings, is better known as Nepal's gateway to the summit of Mount Everest. It is the headquarters of two districts, Solu and Khumbu. Climbing expeditions to the world's tallest peak carry back nostalgic memories of Namche, the last staging post between civilisation and the wild, snow-bound wasteland. The expeditionists recruit Sherpas known all over the world for their loyalty, fortitude and unmatched prowess in carrying heavy backloads to high altitudes.

Namche is situated at an altitude of nearly 9000 feet, an altitude of almost 160 miles north-east of Kathmandu, the capital of Nepal. There used to be no road until the late seventies to the village and the distance had to be trekked over bridle paths. In the sixties, a biweekly air service began to operate between Kathmandu and Lukla airstrip, a good six days' march to Namche.

Riding is another Sherpa village situated at a 11,000-foot altitude at two days' march above Namche on the slopes of Mount Everest. Tang-Burje, a famous monastery, is situated close by. An old Buddhist nun,

76

named Noma Dima, was living in the monastery in 1968, when this scribe trekked to the village. Noma Dima had this experience to narrate:

"I was born unfortunate," she said in her dialect, translated to me by the lamas, who could speak Nepali. "My father died within a week of my birth. The lama counselled my mother to cast me off lest she too might die under the malefic influence of my stars. That was how, as soon as my breast feeding was over, my mother gave me away to Tang Burje, a monastery for nuns. She would drop in twice or thrice a week to have a look at her abandoned baby."

In the monastery, Noma Dima was given all the necessary training to make her a good nun. She learnt reading, writing and arithmetic apart from the discipline of prayer, worship and the system of maintenance of prayer halls. She partook in cooking, fetching water from the stream, washing linen and keeping the monastery neat and tidy. "Life acquired an order and I felt happy."

"The event I am now going to narrate occurred shortly after I turned seventeen. Most of girls of my age had to fetch water. On the day this happened, it was my turn. I got delayed in going out as I was preoccupied in some domestic chores that day. Having already done four trips, I had yet another ten to make. Darkness was gathering all round and I was in a hurry to finish the day's job."

"Just when I got ready to return a fifth time with my load, somebody at my back lifted me up bodily. I felt hard, rough hair grazing my neck and cheeks. As I cast a glance behind, I was dumbfounded at the sight of a ghastly monster. It was a blood-curdling experience. I lost my power to speak or cry aloud. Within moments, I fell unconscious and I can hardly recollect how long I remained in stupor."

"As I came around, I found myself prostrate on a rock shared by a hideous creature whose sight sent me shivering. He moved his hard, dirty finger over my brows and face; brought them close to my nostrils to feel if I was breathing and really alive."

"Finding me alive, he lifted me afresh as if I was a bag of sugar. For nearly half an hour, he carried me on his back till he unloaded me afresh on a rock. A dense bush appeared within sight. He bade me walk towards the bush. I was imprisoned inside it all night, lying on a stony surface amid the stench of unbearable, rotten flesh, which seemed it would blow off my head any moment."

"I was shivering with cold. The weird creature pressed me against its hard, hairy body. Scared by the physical contact, I remained a semiconscious captive till the predawn hour when this creature walked away, leaving me all by myself. By now, I felt reassured that he meant no physical harm to me. Nevertheless, I could not forsake my fright."

As the morning grew brighter, I got a clearer view of the filthy hole in which I had had to spend the night almost semiconscious in captivity. I lay in foul stink in a small, dingy cave, probably a natural one. In a corner of the cave lay a heap of skeletons, probably the bones of animals devoured by this creature.

A breakfast delicacy — the snowfrog

"After nearly three hours' absence, he returned with a handful of living frogs in both of his fists. He placed them before me. As he beckoned to me to help myself to a breakfast, I shuddered at the idea though I had seen frogs being eaten earlier. Several starving men in my village would collect frogs but I detested the idea of eating them as I belonged to a wealthy monastery having plenty to eat. While I refused to eat frogs, dead or alive, I saw the creature relishing this diet. Having finished his collection, he patted my face tenderly with his palms and signalled me to sit where I was. He went out afresh. This time, it did not take him long to return. He brought back some wild fruits. I barely had an appetite due to nervousness and fear. Nevertheless, I ate a few fruits. Apparently, this cheered my captor. He did not go out. Throughout the day and the following night, he kept pressing me against his hard, hairy chest. By the next dawn, I had become the unwed wife of my abductor, who was a yeti."

"A few days later, he went out hunting, leaving me alone. When he returned, the body of a large, barking deer, which the monster had killed, hung loosely over his shoulder. He flung it before me, tore it into bits and squeezed its fat. He now massaged my entire body with the fat. It imparted warmth and vitality to my body. He ate its flesh and offered me a share. I had my first taste of raw meat."

"As the days rolled on, I resigned myself to my fate. Most of the time, the yeti sat by me, looking affectionately, touching my face with his hard fingers or combing my hair with his long nails. Expressions on his face reflected his happiness or annoyance. He smiled whenever he saw me eating and once, as a frog jumped off my mouth, he laughed the way an idiot laughs. He did most of the talking by gestures and signs. While patting my cheeks, his throat produced a grating sound like a hubble-bubble's."

The yeti's physique

Noma Dima betrayed no trace of emotion as she described the physique of her abductor. "The creature was exceptionally tall, taller than any man I have ever seen.

He walked on two legs that were shorter in proportion to his huge frame. His feet were not too large and the toes grew far apart. The hands were abnormally long and they touched his knees when he stood erect. His head, unusually small as compared to his huge frame, rose like a coconut shell from the middle of the forehead. But for his face and palms, hands and feet, his entire body was covered with a long, thick overgrowth of hair. With his sharp and long nails, big teeth set on a sturdy jaw, he could tear animals asunder in no time. While walking, he stood erect on two legs like a human being but while climbing a steep rock or a snow-covered mountain, he used all the fours like a monkey. He could climb steep rocks with unimaginable ease and speed. He could leap very high, very wide."

"I had barely spent ten days in the cave when there was a heavy snowfall on the mountain. I felt sick due to the excessive cold. Realising the problem I faced in eating raw flesh, the creature began to bring a kind of root potato which was delicious and gave me warmth and vitality. The supply was soon interrupted because of heavy snowfall in winter. I had no option but to accept his request that I share the frogs he had collected in plenty by turning big boulders along frozen streams."

After nearly a month of her stay with the yeti, Noma Dima said, the creature began to take her out on excursions over the barren snowscape. He leapt with ease from rock to rock, carrying her piggyback. He seemed to take delight in exhibiting his strength by lifting big boulders and hurling them over long distances. "One day, we sighted a bull roaming about on lower ranges relatively free from snow. He beckoned to me to sit and watch as he himself rushed to the bull with great care. I was keenly watching his movements from my perch."

A duel

"As he stood close to the bull, the creature gave a shrill, yelling cry. Before the bull could get ready, the yeti clutched both his horns. The bull and the yeti were engaged in a duel for a few minutes. Whenever the bull tried to raise its head, the yeti forced it down with intense pressure. After a few minutes of trial of strength between the two, the yeti pulled the beast towards a big rock standing behind him. Pulling the bull near its chest, he gave the quadruped a violent jerk which repulsed it several yards back. Its horns now freed, the bull paused a while and the next moment made a terrible charge at the yeti. For a split second, the creature stood motionless till the bull reached within a yard of his arms. He now swiftly stepped aside with the result that the bull's head dashed against the rock. The bull was dead in no time. The yeti now asked me to come down. When I reached the bull, I found its head cracked into two pieces. Both of us shared a meal of its brain and left the rest for other creatures."

Escape from an Avalanche

The yeti always took utmost precautions to ensure her safety. One day when both were wandering along a snow-covered range in search of food, he suddenly gripped her arms and leapt aside into a small ditch in which he kept her head and his own buried tightly against the ground. Instantly, a loud, thunderous sound shook the entire neighbourhood. Within moments an avalanche carrying millions of tonnes of snow and debris came hurtling down. It stopped very close to our hideout. "The creature now pressed his mouth against my lips and started pumping his breath into my lungs. Having down so for nearly a minute, he was on his legs again." "I saw now," Noma Dima said, "the avalanche which could have buried us both had he not protected me in the nick of time". Next, the yeti had also protected her against being choked for avalanches generate temporarily a vast atmospheric vacuum. Those who escape an avalanche usually die of suffocation. A yeti instinctively apprehends the imminent disaster. He gave her timely artificial respiration to avert the worst due to the absence of oxygen supply in the atmosphere.

She Becomes Pregnant

Noma Dima recalled that by now she had spent two winters as her yeti's consort. One day she felt very sick. She did not have fever, yet she felt very weak. She lay in the cave, reluctant to go out. Winter had now come to an end. The yeti brought a fresh supply of her favourite root potato. She had lost her appetite for this too. He brought wild fruits. Though she relished the sour ones, she could eat very little. She felt like vomiting all day and longed to get any fried meal. "I strongly craved for a mouthful of fried maize flour." The yeti was helpless about obtaining any such thing. He appeared to be deeply worried about her ailment. One day he left the cave and did not return all night. She kept awake out of fright. "Next morning," she said, "I saw two figures in the distant snowscape taking big strides toward the cave. When both came close, I saw two yetis but the stranger who came was totally different from my captor. The visitor had long breasts loosely dangling over her nape. It was an aged she-yeti. She spent nearly half an hour examining my body before she went back. When my captor returned after seeing off the visitor, he brought along a few bunches of berries. She relished their sour taste.

"The yeti sat alongside me the entire day. He was in no mood to go out for the usual food collection. In the afternoon, he beckoned to me to follow him. After a three-hour walk, I realised that my village was near at hand. I could recognise it from the colourful banners fluttering on poles around the monastery."

Birth of the Yeti's Son

"When almost a mile's distance was still left, the yeti beckoned to me to walk away to my home and stay with my mother." "I did not feel like parting with my first man", Noma Dima confessed. "Yet he insisted on my return to my mother's home as he held forth assurances of visiting me from time to time. That was what I could comprehend from his gestures." "As I parted, he kept standing on a rock. When I turned the corner, I guessed he had already left for his cave."

Noma Dima found her mother cooking dinner when she entered her home. "She was stunned to see me attired in deerskin. I narrated to her the entire sequence of my bizarre adventures with the grotesque biped of the snowland."

Six months later, Noma Dima said she gave birth to a male baby. It was a freak child. Long wool-like hair covered his entire body. He had the anatomy of a human being and the face of a monkey. Along with his broad chest, he had long hands and short legs. "During this entire period, its father repeatedly called on me, exercising utmost caution to escape the notice of villagers. He would sneak in whenever my mother was away. With his strong sense of hearing, he perceived the sound of footsteps of the approaching person and fled before anyone could enter our home."

The village folk detested yetis. It was the common belief that any person who saw a yeti was certain to meet instant death. Fearing the worst, I warned him against paying us a visit. "I entreated him not to come by assuring him that I would rejoin him once the baby could walk. I warned the yeti not to touch his baby as he was too weak. On the contrary, he liked to fondle him with his hard fingers and ran his rough palm all over his delicate hairy skin. Every time, he came, he brought fruit for me and his baby."

Noma Dima said one trait that she marked in particular was the long, hairy monster's fright of the burning lamp. She would blow off the light to make him feel at home. "He disliked a hot meal and preferred to eat it cold. He wouldn't dare enter the kitchen and would refuse to enter my room till I put off the fire meant to warm it up."

"As the child grew up satisfactorily in my mother's home, I rejoined the monastery to attend to the usual chores. When the child became two years" old, he began to utter queer sounds in his attempts to speak. His speech did not resemble human children's. He just yelled like his father. He had remarkable strength for a child of his age. He could lift a grinding-stone by one hand."

"Equally remarkable was his sense of hearing. While we would know of his father's arrival by the knock at the door, the child could anticipate it fifteen minutes in advance. He liked his father's presence and would refuse to part when it was time for the yeti to leave. He possessed a remarkable visual power which enabled him to see in the dark. He liked to eat meals raw and cold instead of those cooked hot."

Noma Dima confided to her mother about the secret visits of the yeti. Though she (her mother) considered it ominous for the family and the village, she maintained an uneasy silence and would sit guard when he was inside.

The birth of Noma Dima's son no longer remained a secret. It was bruited around all over the village that she had escaped the yeti's captivity. The head lama of the monastery had no objection to her employment. He recalled several instances of childbirth from the yeti's union with human females. Also, he was aware of the popular superstition that an untimely end awaited anyone who saw a yeti.

The boy was now running into his fourth year. The yeti insisted on our return to his cave. He explained to her through his odd gibberish speech that the boy would be spoilt in human society. He would like him to lead a yeti's free life. One night, he sat longer, planning her return to the cave with their son. It was shortly before dawn that a villager chanced to see him in the village street, trying to make an escape. He raised a loud alarm which attracted many in the village. By this time, the villager had fallen unconscious. He did not come around.

"Panic and alarm gripped the entire village. People feared everyone would die one after another as sequel to the yeti's uninterrupted visits. They approached the head lama who called on us at the head of an angry mob. He tried to ascertain from me and my mother if the yeti had visited our home the previous night." Noma Dima expressed her ignorance but the lama got to know from her son about his fathers visit. The lama warned her to either leave the village or stop the visits of the yeti. They threatened to kill the yeti if he was sighted next time.

Worried about the life and safety of the yeti, Noma Dima warned him against the villagers' threat. She disclosed that, to avert the tragedy, she had even toyed with the idea of returning to cave life but she did not like it at heart since she wanted her child to grow up and get the benefit of instruction at the lamasery. This course too posed certain risks. Her son's presence offended the village boys.

Though far more strong than any child of his age, her son was occasionally stoned or beaten up with sticks by street urchins. Several times, he returned home injured. He reacted violently to such physical attacks. Not unoften, he would cripple boys twice his age. Even elders were frightened of his presence. They feared his stay would bring misfortune to the entire village people. Already, crops had failed successively for the past three years. The village people were now blaming her son for this calamity.

Noma Dima now considered it her prime responsibility to warn her yeti-husband. She awaited his visit on several nights on the dark route he usually took to the village. He failed to turn up.

He came eight days later when she had withdrawn her guard. By now the villagers had posted guards on all the approach routes to the mountain hamlet.

Noma Dima was caught unawares when the yeti peeped indoors at her home one dark night. She hurried to warn him and asked him to go back instantly. He refused to leave without fondling his son for a few minutes. He had already been sighted by the village guards. Within no time, he was attacked by an angry mob carrying flaming torches and deadly weapons. The yeti was hardly scared of weapons but he lost his nerve at the sight of the flares. The villagers now began to hurl their weapons on him. He sustained injuries in different part of his body. In his bid to escape, he leapt into a deep crevasse. The villagers were now reassured that he must have died after falling from a steep height.

She remained worried as the yeti did not show up for the next few days. Her heart thumped at the thought of her yeti-husband's death. But he returned a full fort night after the chase. He dropped in silently. He caressed her face and kissed the sleeping boy. He looked too weak with several burn injuries and bruises all over his body. One of his legs had got crippled as he had slipped into the crevasse. He made entreaties that she return his son in case she herself did not like to go out to live with him.

Noma Dima insisted on retaining her son. At this he remained sitting for some time. Suddenly, tears started flowing down his cheeks. He kissed her and said he was leaving. He got up and took the boy in his arms. Before she had the time to know what was transpiring, he tore the boy into bits. Within the twinkling of an eye, the living child was turned into a heap of flesh and bones. "Before I could utter a word, he rushed out. I had lost both my son and my husband."

"The following morning, the villagers brought the news that the charred, dead body of a yeti bearing many marks of burns and stab injuries had been found in the stream below."

Part III
Appendices

Appendix-1

Excerpts from Brian S. N. Ashkenazi's Letter captioned 'Goongi the Yeti' reproduced in *The Times of India*, New Delhi, 6 August 1979.

Brian S. N. Ashkenazi writes that he had sighted from the rear an exceptionally tall tribal near the railway station yard at Peshawar Cantonment way back in the thirties. He saw the tribal collecting edibles from a heap of garbage. His body was covered with dark, thick hair. Local people told him [the writer] that similar tribals frequently visited the outskirts of the town to collect food. They never harmed human beings. People called them *jangli admi* (forest men).

What's called the abominable snowman, the yeti, Bigfoot, Sasquatch and so on was seen by him [Ashkenazi] at high altitudes, hunting in the woods near hill stations like Mussoori, Naini Tal, Simla, etc.

The adult male is of gigantic stature, standing between eight and twelve feet tall or more and possessing phenomenal strength and agility. It *[sic]* is usually very dark in colour with thick black hair over most of the body. It has a thick black mane flowing down from the front of its neck to below its navel. Its loins are covered with a skirt-like mass of black hair. It has large canine teeth, a broad nose with very dilated nostrils, a conical head covered with short, shingled hair and its fingernails are usually very long and claw-like, while its feet are prehensile. It is human enough to speak an intelligible language not based on written script, and to be member of a social order of a patriarchal type.

The species which is of cannibalistic origin eats raw meat and uncooked leaves, roots, etc., remains completely unclothed and can see perfectly in pitch darkness. It has a life span of more than 300 years.

Appendix-2

Ashkenazi's Encounter with the *Jangli Admi*

Recalling the Peshawar sighting, Ashkenazi wrote that local people told him that he was a '*jangli admi*', also known as 'Haila', a member of a very wild and bestial tribe, half-man, half-ape from the Pamirs, who came down often at dusk from the foothills to forage for the leftovers of items of food from the dustbin, which he ate. "He was very friendly, I was told, and did no harm to anyone keeping largely to himself. He had once allowed them [the local people] to measure him and he was twelve feet tall. Surprisingly, his toes pointed backwards."

Ashkenazi walked up to the giant, whose back was turned towards him. "I noticed that," he wrote, "he was completely naked but covered almost completely with thick black hair flowing down the nape of his neck and covering his back like that of a black lion, and the hair around his neck was very thick and dense. The top of his head was elongated like a cone and was covered with fuzzy hair. His face was Negroid .... He had flaring nostrils and his forehead sloped sharply backward with a horn-like growth in the middle of it."

"Apparently he could speak but said not a single word, stroking his scraggy goatee with his long left hand. Except for his goatee and prominent sideburns, his face was more or less devoid of much hair."

It was some years later after he [Ashkenazi] had reared a baby yeti that he realised that the "friendly Negroid giant he had met was indeed a real yeti."

Appendix-3
Ashkenazi's Version of Two Yeti Species

Ashkenazi describes two species of the creature. One of them was a baby yeti [female] seduced over a chocolate piece by a tea gardener Richard Watson way back in 1938. He [Ashkenazi] tried to rear her and she travelled with him upto Murree, a hill resort now in Pakistan.

Ashkenazi also cites the account of Mira Behn (Mahatma Gandhi's Irish disciple who settled down in India and spent many years at different places in the Himalaya, including Kumayun), testifying [to] the presence of a smaller species of the creature.

Reproduced in *Indian Express* (Sunday edition), Bombay, 2 February 1981.

Appendix-4

Excerpt from *Naya Sandesh* (Weekly)

The tabloid report (a free translation) stated that Nepal's citizenship certificates were given to mysterious off-spring of the yeti. Therefore, a great deal of curiosity prevailed about the creature. It is not an animal but a *'jangli admi'* (wild forest dweller); not imagination but a fact.

Yetis are found in considerable number in the Ganesh Himal region. In summer they live on the upper ranges of the Himalayas and in winter migrate to its foothills.

According to Hari Bahadur Thapa and Buddhiman Tamang, in [the villages of] Kaironja, Jhaling and Lapa, the progenies of yetis are found in good number. These villages are situated at distances of 100, 60 and 30 miles, respectively, north of Kathmandu. The MPs told the *Naya Sandesh* weekly that there were 110 families in these villages that were progenies of yetis. Their fathers and grandfathers were born of yeti. A prominent hunter of his day, Kaitashi Tamang, now 80, told the journal's reporter that 60 years back, a female yeti had abducted a local villager. He escaped from the she-yeti's custody three years later to his native village and disclosed that

96

by his union with the yeti woman, a son and a daughter were born in her mountain home. The female yeti came to the village after he had escaped from her custody. For a long duration, she persisted in shouting but when no one responded, she killed the daughter then and there, and left her son behind. The offspring of this male child are still in Kaironja. The report also said that the yetis eat a frog called *Manaha*, whose size grows to a human baby's dimension when it is picked up from its hibernation space beneath a rock. The male and female yetis are very tall. They have a big lump of flesh over their shoulders, large ears and a hairy, long body. Their voice reverberates like a tiger's.

In Kaironja, Jhaling and Lapa, the yeti offspring speak the local Tamang dialect. They have got domesticated and acquired Nepali citizenship .... They bear a sense of inferiority complex over being treated as the offpsring of the wild forest man (*jangli admi*). In the local dialect they are called *Dinimang* (ghost of the sun). In these villages, the yeti offspring are causing great deal of trouble to hunters by hitting them with stones and tree trunks. They cannot withstand the smell of explosives. In the foothills of Ganesh Himal, yeti footprints are found November onwards.

The male yeti eats male human beings and the female yeti female human beings, according to a common belief prevalent among villagers.

Appendix-5
Yeti or the Snowman*

Yeti or the 'abominable snowman', as people outside Nepal call it, is found all over the Nepal Himalayas and also in the Himalayas in India and beyond. According to our belief, they are human-like creatures, who live above the snowline, are very powerful and can move very swiftly on steep ascents of tough, snow-clad mountains that are beyond the climbing prowess of human beings. They have been known to us; by us, I mean people living on the Himalayan side of Nepal, and we believe in the existence of the creature. We regard them as very sacred and we never try to injure or harm them in any way. Sherpas and Lepchas, who have their villages on high Himalayan slopes, are very much scared of this creature and mostly they believe the sight of a yeti as very inauspicious for their own selves and their families. It may be just a coincidence that whenever some Sherpa saw any yeti, he had some misfortune in the form of his own prolonged illness or of his relative's death.

---

*Recomposed by Rev Lama Punyabajra, Chief Monk of HH Dalai Lama's monastery at Bauddha, Kathmandu.

On the Yeti Trail

According to Sherpa belief, the best way of avoiding bad luck after sighting a yeti was to keep the matter to one's own self and not to speak about it to anyone. This is why the Sherpas are always very much afraid of talking about the yeti, especially to foreigners. They are afraid of the thought that by passing the information, the yeti would be killed by the foreigners and this could invite trouble for their family. We, the lamas, who live on the highest snowline of the Himalayas, never try to face any yeti so as to avoid bad luck. If by chance we see them, we return to perform special *pujas* (prayers) as a precaution against any mishap. There are many reliable and trustworthy accounts of personal sightings of a yeti by highly respectable lamas.

About 50 years ago, when the Sherpa villages were very few and there were thick forests on the snowline, the yetis abounded in numbers and it was a problem in those days to protect farms. The entire days, labour by Sherpas in their field was spoilt by hordes of yetis during the night. They used to imitate [farmers] working on farms, having watched the operations the entire day, while hiding in the woods. The Sherpas had to think of some way of getting rid of these creatures who were far more powerful than the natives. Taking advantage of the imitating habits of the yetis, the Sherpas, under the keen watchful eyes of the yetis in the woods, drank a lot of alcohol and instead of working on the fields, exchanged angry words among themselves. While retiring at sunset, they left alcoholic drinks and poisoned swords in their fields. During the night, the yetis, thus, according to their habits of imitating men, took a lot of drinks. They charged at each other with swords and brought an end to themselves. The Sherpas thus got relieved of the yetis in their respective villages.

Although most yetis have been killed during the past

50 years, many are still left and occasionally reported seen in areas around Helumbu and Melumche, where I have my monasteries and summer camps. Many of my family members have seen them and once my eldest son, when nearly ten, escaped from being kidnapped by a yeti at Helumbu.

According to my careful survey of the yetis, they are of three kinds: (1) Nyalmo; (2) Rimi and (3) Racksi Bompo.

The Nyalmo is the biggest and the most powerful among these species. Usually, it lives in forests located at over 10,000 feet. Its body is covered with long hair, two to three inches long. It has a muscular body, possessing the strength of about ten to fifteen men together. The face is flat like ape's with deep sunken eyes; the arms reach up to the knees; and, the strong and stout legs end in feet having four toes turned backwards. Nyalmos have a conical head which is without a forehead. This type is fast disappearing. Very few of them are left now in the Himalayas. They are carnivorous and are often reported having killed yaks, sheep, goats and even bears in order to eat. They have been observed by people celebrating community feasts under big pine trees on full-moon nights.

Female yetis are found leading the groups and they are probably the leaders of their society. These Nyalmos are so powerful that they can throw big rocks weighing over 200 pounds to a distance of 100 yards. Their footprints, 18 to 20 inches long, have been many times marked and photographed by different Himalayan mountaineering teams. It is very difficult to capture a Nyalmo. They have been reported having sexual relations with human beings. As a matter of fact, there is a Nyalmo family in village Tarke, born of a Nyalmo mother and a Sherpa father. They are abnormally tall, hairy, monkey-shaped and wild natured. We call them the Nyalmo family.

The Rimis are maximum ten-foot tall, hairy, ape-shaped and both vegetarian and carnivorous. They are mostly found in Barun Valley between the Everest and Makalu ranges and are equally difficult to capture. They too have often been reported having sex with human beings and are friendly to their opposite human sex.

The Racksi Bompo are the type found in large numbers around Helumbu and can be easily captured. They are of human stature, four to five-feet tall, all hairy. They have stout legs, long arms and wrinkled faces like an orangutan's and they sometimes walk on all fours. They are very fond of maize, millet and other cornflours. They raid potato crops and often invade lonely houses for vegetables and salt. The Sherpas have great respect for them otherwise it would be very easy to entrap a Racksi Bompo.

It was this kind of a yeti which once tried to kidnap my ten-year-old son when he was one day playing till late in the evening outside my summer camp at Melumche. Before the yeti could reach my son, who remembers the event quite well, he saw the former and shouted for help. The yeti ran away, having found my son alert and shouting.

One playmate of my daughter, called Yalo-Yuli, was taken away by a Racksi Bompo when she was nearly six years old. Living with the yeti for several years, she could understand the yeti language which was nothing more than monkey talk. She was one day found moving on all her fours in front of her parents' home and it took her a full two years to revert to human ways. When I saw her, she had forgotten most of the yeti language and was very sick. At that time it was hardly conceived that one day a scientific research may begin on the yeti. Hence, I took no notice of her case. She expired later after a long illness. Much information about her could still be gathered from her relatives who know of the incident.

My son Ganesh Bajra organised a 50-man search party last autumn for the yetis and collected much valuable information about them. Although they are like human beings, they do not know how to build their house. As such, they dwell usually in caves or under hanging boulders. They don't know about clothes and are most primitive in the sense that they don't have any weapons, not even a club which the primitive, prehistoric man was supposed to possess. They do not know how to make a fire and were mighty scared of its sight, like any other animal. They are more primitive than the prehistoric caveman and are a very interesting subject of study for the anthropologists. My son has discovered several caves where these Racksi Bompos live; and, if someone likes, they can be caught with the permission of the Nepal Government. No Sherpa will ever like to cooperate in the catch of a yeti except those who have lived long with foreigners in connection with expeditions and are educated enough to distrust the superstitions about the sight of a yeti.

I have read with keen interest about the proposed expedition for the search of a yeti arriving this month under the leadership of Mr. Tom Slick. I have met Mr. Slick last year when he was here in connection with his first inconclusive yeti expedition and I assured him of cooperation in his next expedition. While I welcome his team, I don't much like his idea of bringing hounds with him. This will not be liked either by the Sherpas or the lamas living in high monasteries. It will only hurt the sentiments of the people here.

It is high time that a team composed of scientists

and anthropologists was organised to visit my area in the Nepal Himalayas in cooperation with enlightened Sherpas. The team under Tom Slick does not have any scientist. I am fully confident that the day is not far away when the mystery of the yeti will be resolved and add to the knowledge of the development and growth of the human race. I wish the expeditions for the yeti a success. Om Mani Padme Hum.

Appendix-6

Summary of Jeanne Koffman's report on her
expedition in the Caucasus region*

The results of the two unofficial expeditions that were made known in the past two months have once again awakened the interest of the Soviet public in the so-called 'snowman' or 'yeti', reports APN. Enthusiasts maintain that in the mountains of the Caucasus and the Pamirs there is indisputable proof of the existence of the mysterious yeti, known to science as the 'relict humanoid'.

The snowman is of about ordinary human height, sometimes a little taller, has a stooping posture and a squat head resting squarely on his shoulder, a sloping forehand, long arms and fingers and long red fur. The creature emits the strangest sounds — it shrieks and whistles, it bleats and mutters. It is agile and cautious and will not eat twice from the same feeding rack.

That is a rough description of the Caucasian snowman given by Jeanne Koffman, well known scholar, surgeon and member of the USSR Geographic Society. Koffman admits that she has not seen the yeti herself

---

*Published as 'Snowman: Renewed Interest in The USSR, *The Times of India*, 16 May 1978.

but she has listened to many different people describing it and its behaviour.

Strange Goings-on

After the sensation the snowman had caused in the late fifties and early sixties, there was a long period of doubt and disappointment which even affected enthusiasts. Many people gave up further search believing it was a waste of time and energy. Only a few continued research. Jeanne Koffman was among them. With a group of volunteer assistants she set out every year for the uninhabited areas of the northern Caucasus.

In the spring of 1978, like in the preceding years, Koffman's group was working in the northern Caucasus. That year it was the valley of the mountain river Malka some 30 to 40 km from Mount Elbrus that attracted the attention of the investigators. The place was not a random choice. The watchman of the mountaineers' camp told them of the strange goings-on there just before the arrival of the group.

One night, the dogs guarding the house started to bark. They would run off some distance and then return whining pitifully. The watchman assured the newcomers that his brave hounds never acted that way. If it had been a bear they would have barked at it until the bear made off and if it had been human beings, they would not have barked at all. The watchman said he went out on the porch and fired his gun a couple of times but he was afraid to go out into the dark. Several nights later the whole thing was repeated. In the morning, the watchman went for firewood up the slope from which the dogs had run down whining with fear and there he saw the imprint of a bare foot in the snow. The watchman, like most people in those parts, had heard about the existence of "wild forest dweller". After hearing these stories, Koffman decided to set up observation of the area.

Footprints Checked

In the middle of March 1978, a group of local huntsmen and two repairmen stopped at the camp. On the night of 17 March, the hounds acted in a strange way again. Ruslan Shamanov, the sports instructor at the camp, ventured out when he heard the barking and it seemed to him he saw a large figure in the darkness. In the morning he went to the place where he thought he had seen the creature and discovered footprints. He called his father and brother and, according to instructions, received from Koffman, they covered the footprints so they would not be washed away by rain and no one would walk over them.

There were 25 imprints altogether but 13 were particularly distinct. They were clearly outlined on firm soil with a large gravel content. Koffman photographed the footprints, measured them and made plaster casts. Making the soil firm with a special glue, she cut out four of the best imprints right out of the ground.

"What is especially surprising", said Koffman, "is the heaviness of the foot. Its length, 25.5 cm is comparatively normal but its breadth is from 12 to 13 cm and the depth of the imprints is from 1.5 cm to 2 cm in hard soil. The size of the creature's stride was from 120 cm to 130 cm which is about twice the size of an average human being. Another curious thing about the imprint is that they follow each other in a straight line as though the creature was walking on a rope." At present, the material collected by Koffman is being analysed by specialists.

Appendix-7

China's Version of Abominable Snowman*

A woman, who looked like a bear, grabbed a Tibetan herdsman and produced two offspring after forcing him to live with her in a Himalayan cave for several years, according to a Canton newspaper, reports Reuter.

The story of the hairy woman and another about a wild man, who held a woman captive in a cave in China's south-western Sichuan Province for 10 years, was recounted in a Canton exhibition about the hunt for the legendary 'abominable snowman', the Yangcheng evening news has reported.

The paper said the Tibetan incident happened in 1964.

When the man escaped from the cave, the hairy woman chased him but was shot by herdsmen. They found the two babies had already been killed by the mother.

In 1960, a woman was carried off by a wild man in Sichuan as she had been washing clothes by a river, the newspaper said. She had two children by him and escaped with them in 1970 after living in a cave.

*The Statesman, New Delhi, 25 October 1984.

Epilogue

Mankind has long awaited in suspense a precise answer to the riddle about the origin and source of the human species. Various categories of scientists even naturalists, anthropologists, and zoologists and geographers and also journalists have 'moved heaven and earth to adduce or sometimes fabricate evidence which would throw light on the nature of that world-wide catastrophe which so transformed the primordial creature's physiognomy that it shed its tail and turned into a two-legged creature endowed with a brain. What were the various phases in the evolution from an ape into man? Is the giant-size monster sighted once in a blue moon in the snow-bound Himalayas the 'missing link' in the evolutionary chain?

Naturalists have classified together a variety of human-like species under the general heading of 'primates'. This group includes such hominids as *Homo ferus* (wild man) and troglodytes (a cave dweller) or a primitive man (who became later the modern man). Have all these species, man excepted, survived? Are they still in existence in certain uninhabited, inaccessible regions unknown to man? Have all the surviving species been identified by naturalists or are some of them still waiting to be discovered? Is the yeti, whose footprints have been sighted up to the mid-eighties in the Nepal Himalayas, now on the verge of extinction or is it dwelling in some isolated stretch of the lofty mountain ranges? Is there a link between the Himalayan yeti, the Chinese snowman and the Caucasus region Almas? Many such questions have been baffling the scientists and other interested groups ever since a Russian explorer sighted a wandering wild man in the mid-nineteenth century in Mongolia.

Evidence about the existence of a primate, so far unknown to science, has been piling up over the past 50 years. Such evidence has originated from a number of countries in both hemispheres, stretching from Alaska to Australia covering both South America and North America and also north-east Siberia. Considering the highly confusing reports and growing public curiosity to know more about the monstrous tailless biped, governments, universities and scientific institutions in a few advanced countries have engaged explorers to undertake field investigations to search for and identify this primate. Mountaineers of repute, who have nothing to gain by mystifying or exaggerating the enigma surrounding the bizarre creature, have testified to sighting giant-size footprints on snow left behind by a biped in a single file for miles on a stretch on the Himalayan snowscapes. The indentations could not have been made on that desolate terrain by any animal other than a biped. The Himalayan bear is ruled out. Even if one were to imagine that this bear was walking on its hind legs, it is not known to do so at such altitudes. Nor can it trudge for miles on end on its hind legs. If a *hominoid* exists on the high Himalayas, how close is its physiognomy to *Homo sapien's*? What does it feed on and how does it subsist all by itself in such a barren and inhospitable terrain?

The yeti-watchers the world over are divided into two camps. On the one hand, there are the non-believers, who attribute the creature to Himalayan folklore and Buddhist mythology and on the other, many naturalists who think, on the strength of the altogether rare sighting of footprints on snow, that the elusive biped could probably be 'the missing link' in the evolution of *Homo sapiens.*

The exploration of the earth's surface is not yet completely over. Many a remote and inaccessible region still remains unknown to man. Again, many creatures ranging from insects to mammals have not yet come to light in the world of the naturalists, although the past 150 years have witnessed the discovery of a large number of creatures unknown earlier.

The discoveries of living primates in modern times owe a lot to the pioneering studies of Professor Boris Porshnev of the former USSR (now Commonwealth of Independent States or CIS). The publication of several of his research papers in the 1950s, on the wild man of Caucasus and the Pamirs, gave a fillip to field investigations in his country. The Soviet Academy of Sciences set up a National Commission on the Wild Man in the USSR. Field investigations were launched in an organised and systematic manner from 1958 onwards to analyse the various aspects of the existence of the strange man like creature known as Almas in the Caucasus region. For about 20 years Professor Jeanne Koffman directed the field researches to settle the question of the vexed identity of the 'wild man' encountered by the explorers and tourists from time to time. Her findings were published in 1978 (see Appendix 6 for a press summary).

On the Yeti Trail

Coming to the Himalayas, the height of the tallest yeti in these mountains was estimated at 12 feet while that in the Caucasus it could have been 5 feet six inches. The size of the footstep in the Nepal Himalayas (13¾" x 6¾") found by Lord Hunt in 1978 in the Everest region is smaller than its Chinese counterpart's (15¼" to 18¾"). In the Pamirs, Russian teams measured them at 13¼" x 6¼" in 1979 and 15¼" x 18¾" in 1981. According to Koffman's data the length of the foot is 25.5 cm (nearly 10.2"), the breadth 12 to 13 cm (i.e. 4.8" to 5.2") and the depth from 1.5 cm to 2 cm (i.e., 0.6" to 0.9"). The length was 'comparatively normal but its breadth' appeared to indicate a size larger than a tall human being's. The size of the creature's stride was from 120 cm to 130 cm (4' to 4'4"), which is about twice the size of an average human being's. Could these imprints have been left by creatures of identical species?

The idea that the Neanderthal species, i.e., *Homo sapiens*, moved out of Europe towards Asian regions appealed to Porshnev. The primitive man had variants of this species in different regions and climes. These variants existed far apart and evolved simultaneously. It is a prehistoric fact that certain species ceased to evolve. Also, it is probable that after a period of growth, which may have stretched into millions of years, there was a throwback in the evolution of some species in certain secluded regions where they may still be in existence. Could it be that the footprints sighted in Caucasus belong to a survivor of the now extinct Neanderthal species?

Naturalists claim that the *Homo gigantopithecus* is a more primitive species of *Homo erectus*, than Neanderthal man. The footprints in the Himalayas belong to an ape-like rather than a man-like creature. It seems to be within the realm of probability that the footsteps sighted

111

in the Himalayas by Lord Hunt, Don Whillans, Doug Houston and other veteran climbers belong to a large ape.

More information is now available on the primitive caveman's settlements in the snow-clad Pamirs in Professor Myra Shackley's book *Still Living* (printed in Hungary, first published English edition, 1983, in the USA) which contains a wealth of scientific data on the yeti, Sasquatch and the Neanderthal enigma.

The outome of field investigations in the remote areas of Russia is still not fully known. Yeti explorers have been gradually turning to the somewhat more accessible Himalayas, to Nepal in particular, where excursions to some of the highest mountain ranges are subject to payment of royalty in hard currency. Sherpas sometimes resort to playing hoaxes in the name of yeti on gullible Western explorers to eke out their livelihood.

It would be presumptuous to claim that the monster whose footprints, or shadowy silhouettes have been glimpsed invariably from a distance by tourists, *sadhus* pilgrims, mountaineers or explorers in Nepal's high-altitude ranges belings to a species of hominids. Does this creature really exist? That is no longer the core issue now. Today, one cannot definitely state that this is a creature belonging to the folklore of Sherpa monasteries. No doubt, the rational scientist will not accept the fact of its existence until it has been found in flesh and blood but no scientist can dismiss the existence of such a creature after analysing the available evidence of its sightings, its footprints on snow, its hair, its droppings in the cave and now the first-person accounts presented in this book.

The analysis of the mysterious creature's hair, droppings, dried scalp and skeletal hand (taken away by Western explorers for laboratory tests) disclosed that they belong to a species as yet unclassified by science. Hence, all the evidence one can bank upon consists of footprints on snow. Several non-believers among mountaineers contend that the indentations could be ascribed to a species of Himalayan bear. The imprints of its sole and toes would get enlarged due to the melting of snow around them. Modern explorers have expressed the view that there is the greater likelihood of these footprints belonging to a giant-size ape rather than to a hominid or Himalayan bear.

If the yeti were a species of primitive or prehistoric man its voice should resemble a human being's. What's the evidence like on this score? Ashkenazi's account reveals that the baby yeti he was rearing was unable to articulate human speech. The unclothed, abnormally tall human-like creature (jangli admi) he sighted from a distance near the Peshawar Cantonment railway station was also incapable of making intonations of human voice. In terms of biology, the baby yeti belongs to the species of man-like ape and the jangli admi to the species of hominid.

The large Himalayan yeti is omnivorous. The most significant factor is that this yeti cannot make fire; in fact, it dreads fire. It does not know how to make tools or use even a tree trunk to attack its foes or defend itself. The yeti cannot be considered a cousin of Neanderthal man who had begun to make both tools and fire. According to fossil finds, the Neanderthal man buried his dead. Like the yeti, he took care of the sick and the aged. He had a social sense. The yeti is also endowed with the faculty of night vision, an attribute of certain species of animals. The yeti can be encountered only by chance as it moves out mainly at night (Hominid nocturna as it is called by naturalists). According to Ashkenazi, who encountered it as recently as the early eighties in the Kashmir Himalayas, the creature has an

113

instinctive sense of tracking leylines through whose help (Ashkenazi explains) it can locate subterranean streams and their intersections. These instinctive qualities are also attributes of certain species of animals.

The male Himalayan yeti has, according to individual testimonies, a fancy for human females but it may pose a danger to males. It has an instinctive premonition of an impending avalanche. The male yeti fondles and caresses the maiden it elopes with. The yeti is a cave-dweller having a strong possessive instinct for the female it has abducted and watches and guards her against rivals. It behaves in a gentle manner with its female consort. One of the females, who had been abducted, told M. M. Gupta (on regaining freedom) that she could read expressions of happiness or irritation on the face of her captor. It can understand her language. It is familiar with mountain tracks leading to human settlements from where it had abducted its female consort. By all accounts, it is endowed with a measure of intelligence unknown among animals.

What distinguishes the primate that evolved into a Neanderthal man from an ape-like man is the former's ability to make fire, tools and possibly spin wool and produce cotton cloth. The Neanderthal man had learnt to live in groups and could possibly build a house for himself, whereas the Himalayan yeti is a loner. The Neanderthal species was believed to have emerged on earth 136,000 years ago and his line appears to have faded off mysteriously nearly 25,000 years ago. Scientists do not rule out the probability of the survival till date of certain Neanderthal species in several unknown tracts of the earth, like the deep valleys concealed within giant Himalayan ranges. The differences in characteristics of the Neanderthal man's physiognomy and those of the abominable snowman's place them in distinctly separate classes.

The yeti with its three distinct sizes (see Chapter 2) is a well-marked species found in the Himalayas in Nepal, Tibet and Sikkim.

In at least two instances, the yeti had been killed, once at Tadadege in Arunachal Pradesh and, on another occasion, in Mustang in Nepal. That establishes its real identity. Though the scientists would like to see the yeti dead or alive, its killing offends popular sentiment in Nepal.

The offspring of the union between the yeti and human females (limited to a few mountain tribes in Nepal) bring out the fact of its existence. The yeti's progeny is also unable to articulate human speech. Its body is hairy and its face resembles an ape's. These progeny grow to the stature of their giant-size male parent. The village community shuns them and calls them by a pejorative term, *Dinimang* (ghost of the sun). They are treated as pariahs. The three villages peopled by members of this hybrid strain (half-man, half-beast) are located at a distance of 100 miles (160 km) north of Kathmandu. The locations are remote and inaccessible. Their (the hybrid strain's) existence was first reported in the early sixties by Kathmandu's English daily *The Commoner*. The Kathmandu language tabloid *Naya Sandesh* weekly's report in the late seventies relies on the version of the National Panchayat members from constituencies ensconsing these villages. They came into focus when the cross-breeds demanded citizenship certificates from the local Panchayat authorities. To the scientist, the offspring of the union of a male yeti and a female human being would certainly be a biological abnormality. To the local village community, they appear to be a biological deformity.

Going by individual testimonies, the height of the different species of the Himalayan yeti ranges from 4 to

12 feet. Footprints on snow reveal four distinct toes with a fifth splayed or backturned. The yeti's small, egg-shaped head rises conically upwards from prominent eyebrow ridges below a mound at the centre of the forehead. The flat face resembles a monkey's. The skin is black or grey. The nostrils under a stunted nose are dilated and the lips too thin to be visible. The chin recedes backward from the large mouth. Earlobes stick out on either side of the temple. The entire body is covered with a thick overgrowth of black or grey hair. (Accounts from Nepal do not report red fur on the yeti's body though a coat of this colour may be an exception, if one is found.) The shoulders carry humps and the arms are disproportionately long. They reach down to the knees as the yeti moves about, swinging them. The legs are disproportionately short as compared to the entire body. The medium sized Himalayan yeti, roughly 5' 6" in height preys upon yak, livestock and corn in the fields. The shortest yeti 4' to 5' tall, usually steals corn and attacks man and livestock. An instance of cross-breeding between a female yeti and male human being had also been reported from Sichuan province of China (contiguous to the eastern boundary of Tibet). It was found that the mother had killed two of her babies.

A few of the more suitable locations for mounting yeti-tracking expeditions are to be found in the commonwealth of Independent States in the Caucasus and the Pamirs. It is believed that Dr. Jeanne Koffman has made certain case studies of the sightings of the wild man and its footprints. In the USA, too, a research institution has been conducting scientific investigations on this strange creature called Bigfoot or Sasquatch. It has been glimpsed, though on very rare occasions, in the Rockies between north California and British Columbia. Scientists have not given a clean chit to Roger Patterson's photograph of a female Sasquatch noticed escaping into the woods at Bluff Creek, California. A still shot by Patterson, this photograph was published in Indian dailies too in the late sixties.

More intensive research has been conducted in China. A large preserve has been set apart in Shenmongjia forest for research on the yeti. A number of sightings of a yeti-like creature were reported 20 to 30 years back from this isolated area lying in the Hubei province.

Explorers in the West view the 'elusive legend' as one of the last few among the earth's major mysteries. On finding this creature, they may put to test the validity of Darwin's theory of natural selection. The ultimate purpose of the search is to ascertain if a link really exists between the *Homo sapiens* (living modern man) and this creature, i.e., if it is a variation of man's original ancestor. If not, does it (the ape-like creature) belong to some other genus? If so, what accounts for its giant stature?

Following the failure of the 1978 attempt (in Sikkim) to photograph the yeti, further search operations in the Himalayas had virtually come to a standstill. Failure had not, however, blunted the explorers' spirit of adventure; indeed, fresh sightings had whetted it. In September 1992, footprints of another mystery snowman, nicknamed 'Yegor' by a local journalist in Petrozavodsk (Karelia, in CIS) were claimed to have been found by him. According to a DPA (German news agency) report quoting Tass (Russian news agency), Victor Serikov a pensioner and three of his friends, who had gone out fishing on the banks of Svetloe lake, around 50 km from the Karelian capital Petrozavodsk, found footprints of an unidentified creature on the soil. They said when they went to their car to have a cup of tea, they found that their thermos flask of tea and a packet of biscuits and sweets had vanished from the back seat. The fishermen found pieces of the broken flask nearby and next to them the huge footprints of an unidentified creature. Serikov make a template of the footprints which was 41 cm long and 20 cm wide. It was identical with the snowman reputed to be living at high altitude in the Himalayas.

Every sighting has spurred a revival in the search for the mysterious creature. According to a London *Times* report (reproduced in *The Statesman*, New Delhi, 18 April 1993) the BBC plans to telecast a film on the abominable snowman in its travelogue series made by Michael Palin, an actor and explorer.

BBC was expected to sponsor an expedition which was scheduled to embark in February 1994 on a 3000-mile journey across the Himalayas and also along the snowy wastes of Canada. This expedition would have a camera crew of eight and would be led by Brian Blessed, 57, another actor and explorer. The planning for the expedition had begun in April 1993. Blessed is expected to mount a separate expedition to Mount Everest in August 1994. He asserted that the series 'could help fulfil a deep contemporary need for adventure and myth'.

To categorically state that the large Himalayan yeti does not exist would be wrong. One reason why it has not been seen so far possibly lies in the fact that it fights shy of human presence and stirs out for preying only after sunset. It would be nearer to reality to concede that the yeti's hideouts are located in regions so inaccessible that it had not been possible to see it; or else because its number had dwindled to such a small size that its species was now on the verge of extinction. For the explorer today, it is mainly a question of tracking the yeti down by its trail on snow. Until it is actually found, it is best to keep one's mind open. In admitting its existence, one has to make a choice between what one has seen with one's eyes and the taunts or derision of sceptics demanding concrete proof of its existence. Hence, to prove themselves right, the believers have to await the outcome of more intensive and purposive field investigations. The gap cannot be bridged by exhibiting faked, unsubstantiated finds like the yeti's scalp or its skeletal hand meant to stir up sensation in the media world.

Select Bibliography

Books Consulted

1. Broughton, Geoffrey, *Climbing Everest*,
   Oxford University Press, Oxford, 1960.
2. Cavendish Richard (ed.),
   Encyclopaedia of the Unexplained: Magic,
   Occultism and Parapsychology, Routledge and Kegan Paul,
   London, 1974.
3. Gurung Harka, *Annapurna to Dhaulagiri*, HMG Nepal,
   Kathmandu, 1968.
4. Herzog, Maurice, *Annapurna*, Jonathan Cape, London, 1952.
5. Hunt, Lord John, *The Ascent of Everest,* Hodder and
   Stoughton, London, 1955.
6. Ratzec, Vladimir, *The Riddle of the Abominable Snowman*,
   Tashkent (Circulated by *Tass*).
7. Stonor, Charles *The Sherpa and the Snowman*, Hollis and
   Carter, London, 1955.
8. Stackley, Myra, *Still Living*, Thames and Hadson, New
   York, 1983.

Journals And Newspapers

1. Ashkenazi, Brian S.N., *Sunday Dispatch*, London, cited in
   The Indian Express, Bombay, 2 February 1981.
2. MacInnes, Hamish, *The Abominable Myth*, Burmah Shell
   News, Vol. VIII, No. 1, 1959.
3. *Kosmolskaya Gazeta* (a Soviet youth Newspaper).
4. *Socialist Industry,* (a Russian Journal)
5. *The Free Press Journal,* Bombay,
6. *The Indian Express*, Bombay and New Delhi.
7. *The Hindustan Times*, New Delhi.
8. *The Statesman*, New Delhi.
9. *The Times of India*, New Delhi.